SELF-CARE in a
CRAZY WORLD

How to Thrive When
Things Get Tough

MARK CARPENTER, M.A, LPC-MHSP
and TYLER ORR, M.A, LPC-MHSP

Self-Care in a Crazy World

ISBN - 978-1-7364890-0-0 *(Paperback)*

Editing, cover design, and formatting by ChristianEditingServices.com

SELF-CARE in a CRAZY WORLD

How to Thrive When Things Get Tough

Contents

Chapter 1 →

Learning to Cope . . .
No, Thrive

"The Father is with me. I've told you all this so that
trusting me, you will be unshakable and assured,
deeply at peace. In this godless world you will
continue to experience difficulties. But take heart!
I've conquered the world."

— JOHN 16:32–33

Consider it a sheer gift, friends, when tests and
challenges come at you from all sides. You know
that under pressure, your faith-life is forced into
the open and shows its true colors. So don't try to
get out of anything prematurely. Let it do its work
so you become mature and well-developed, not
deficient in any way.

— JAMES 1:2–4

This book came together in 2020. The year of a pandemic, social
unrest, political confusion, and, in my area (Chattanooga,
Tennessee), a tornado. This has been a tough year for all of
us. It has been hard to find stability emotionally, physically,
and relationally. The constant onslaught of uncertainty, stress,

and conflict has brought a fatigue. I think God has designed all of us to deal with transitory stress, or stress that comes and goes, but not stress that lingers for months on end. This year has produced a fatigue that is affecting everyone's life. It is perfectly normal to feel exhausted and overwhelmed when dealing with the emotions that come from prolonged stress and uncertainty. For some people this fatigue looks just like a low-grade depression in which they struggle with focus and concentration and seem to want to step back further away from life. For others it seems to create an agitation, anger, or reactivity to the world around them. Many feel weary, anxious, powerless, sad, frustrated, and irritable. Do you notice these signs?

- Your eating or sleeping habits have changed, and you've gained or lost weight.

- You have trouble focusing, and sometimes it feels like a brain fog.

- You feel anxious or nervous.

- You feel irritable and snap at or argue with others.

- You have trouble starting or finishing tasks, and you lack motivation.

- You are unable to stop racing thoughts.

- You withdraw or avoid other people and social situations.

I have found these are normal responses to living a life of stress, trauma, conflict, and change. Sadly, I wish this were the experience of only last year, but for most of us it has become normal. This is not a book that applies only to the year of the pandemic.

The year 2020 was so difficult because it seemed to reflect what is becoming normal. We live a life driven by activity, to-do lists, stress, conflict, and anger. Sadly, we have lost touch with what it feels like to sit beside quiet waters (see Psalm 23) or live a life where the burden is light, and the yoke is easy (see Matthew 11:30). That is why you're reading this now; we all need to find some way to bring self-care or order back to our day-to-day world. This hectic, stressful life robs us of peace and joy and creates loss of purpose. We feel lost. The good news is that we can regain purpose and health when we learn to care for ourselves.

I remember as a boy reading James 1:2–4 (see above). The passage says to consider it a gift, or as other translations say, a joy, when you experience tests, trials, challenges, and tribulations. My reaction is the same as it was when I was a boy reading it for the first time: Wow! A gift, a joy. Doesn't that seem a little too much to expect? This is hard. How do we walk with God, coping with the world around us? We have to learn to care for our body, soul, and spirit. Just as we care for the people we love, we have to learn to care for ourselves. The nurture of self-care is difficult when we live in an environment that hinders and even prevents that nurture.

I've been blessed with a healthy body that I can push to accomplish more and more. Sadly, I sometimes push it too far. I've been blessed with a good mind that I use to enjoy the world and the relationships around me, but sometimes I stress my mind with a busyness and a to-do list that seems to never end. I have a spirit in which God lives, but many times my busyness and stress cause me to ignore the strongest part of my life: God's presence in me. I think that is the condition of most people's lives. The busyness, stress, and trauma of the present and the wounds of the past create unbalanced lives.

We live in a world full of constant, hectic pressure, but God designed us to live in a world with transitory stress. He designed us to flow in and out of stress, not live in it. We all have experienced stress from time to time; it's part of the emotional and physical life we live on this side of heaven. Our stressors have many sources—our circumstances, bodies, thoughts, and the way we view and interact with the world around us. It is natural to feel stressed at moments of pressure and conflict.

If you're living with high levels of stress that don't go away, you're putting your well-being at risk. The stress degrades your emotional and physical health and distorts your ability to think clearly, function effectively, and enjoy life. The Mayo Clinic states this about chronic stress:

> The long-term activation of the stress-response system and the overexposure to cortisol and other stress hormones that follows can disrupt almost all your body's processes. This puts you at increased risk of many health problems, including
>
> - Anxiety
>
> - Depression
>
> - Digestive problems
>
> - Headaches
>
> - Heart disease
>
> - Sleep problems
>
> - Weight gain
>
> - Memory and concentration impairment (Mayo Clinic, 2019)

If stress is part of the human condition, then what are our options? Self-care is learning how to care for ourselves in a way that increases our capacity to deal with life and develops increased resilience. Our activities of self-care should be simple but effective for our body, soul, and spirit. They should protect and guard our heart (see Proverbs 4:23) and should be gentle to our mind and body.

If you don't live a balanced life, this human condition of stress, conflict, and struggle can affect your resilience. Resilience is the ability to be stretched and pulled but still come back to who you are, to your original shape, emotionally, spiritually, and relationally. Think of resilience as a rubber band; if you pull and stretch it, even if it's sometimes abused, it returns to its original shape. That is the metaphor for each of us. If we are stretched, pulled, and maybe abused, is there something that can help us return to our original shape? That help comes from the skills you'll learn in this book, what I call self-care built around healthy relationships.

There is a wealth of research and options for self-care. The Centers for Disease Control and Prevention says that coping with stress in a healthy way will make you, the people you care about, and your community stronger. Stress can cause some of the following:

* Fear and worry about your own health and the health of your loved ones, your financial situation or job, or loss of support services you rely on

* Changes in sleep or eating patterns

* Difficulty sleeping or concentrating

* Worsening of chronic health problems

- Worsening of mental health conditions

- Increased use of tobacco, alcohol, and other substances

Here are some healthy ways to cope with stress:

- Know where and how to get treatment and other support services and resources, including counseling or therapy (in person or through telehealth services).

- Take care of your emotional health to help you think clearly and react to urgent needs to protect yourself and your family.

- Take breaks from watching, reading, or listening to news stories, including those on social media. Hearing about the pandemic repeatedly can be upsetting.

- Take care of your body.

  o Take deep breaths, stretch, or meditate on God's Word.

  o Try to eat healthy, well-balanced meals.

  o Exercise regularly.

  o Get plenty of sleep.

  o Avoid excessive alcohol and drug use.

- Make time to unwind. Try to do some activities you enjoy.

- Connect with others. Talk with people you trust about your concerns and how you are feeling.

- Connect with your community or faith-based organizations. Consider connecting online, through social media, or by phone or mail.

The more I walk and work with people, the more clearly I see that God designed us with a body, soul, heart, and spirit that make up our whole being. The fascinating aspect is that He created those parts of us to love and serve Him (see **Mark 12:30; 1 Thessalonians 5:23**), and they all need care that only we can provide for ourselves. No one can do it for us. We have to develop habits and skills to care for our body, soul, and spirit. I think we can even see demonstrations of self-care in Scripture. Here are three examples.

1) Jesus said, "Are you tired? Worn out? Burned out on religion? Come to me. Get away with me and you'll recover your life. I'll show you how to take a real rest. Walk with me and work with me—watch how I do it. Learn the unforced rhythms of grace. I won't lay anything heavy or ill-fitting on you. Keep company with me and you'll learn to live freely and lightly." (Matthew 11:28–30)

This is one of my favorite scriptures. When I am tired and worn out, it gives me permission to let go of control. I need reminding that someone greater than I am is truly in control and cares for me. This passage seems to imply that my heart can get weary, and time with God in the rhythms of His grace can empower and refuel me.

2) When Elijah saw how things were, he ran for dear life to Beersheba, far in the south of Judah. He left his young servant there and then went on into the desert another day's journey. He came to a lone broom bush and collapsed in its shade, wanting in the worst way to be done with it all—to just die: "Enough of this, GOD! Take my life—I'm ready to join my ancestors in the grave!" Exhausted, he fell asleep under the lone broom bush.

Suddenly an angel shook him awake and said, "Get up and eat!"

He looked around and, to his surprise, right by his head were a loaf of bread baked on some coals and a jug of water. He ate the meal and went back to sleep.

The angel of GOD came back, shook him awake again, and said, "Get up and eat some more—you've got a long journey ahead of you."

He got up, ate and drank his fill, and set out. Nourished by that meal, he walked forty days and nights, all the way to the mountain of God, to Horeb. When he got there, he crawled into a cave and went to sleep. (1 Kings 19:3–9)

The fascinating thing about this passage is the emphasis on how Elijah's emotional and spiritual needs are connected to his physical needs. God doesn't answer his cry or concerns; He just gives him food and rest. God seems to say a snack and a nap will help you cope and understand.

3) As often as possible Jesus withdrew to out-of-the-way places for prayer. (Luke 5:16)

I am in awe that even Jesus needed and wanted to pray to refresh His spirit. The model He shows us is that we need to find balance and time with God.

The chapters ahead will give you practical ways to increase your capacity to deal with stress, trauma, and your busy life. Here are seven quick self-care tips to get you started before you dive into the rest of the book.

1. **Develop good nutrition habits.** Stressed people often eat emotionally, consuming too many carbs and

sugars. This pattern handicaps your body's ability to cope. If regular meals are difficult, try to keep a stash of healthy, protein-packed snacks on hand.

2. **Exercise.** Increase your heart rate for more than twenty minutes four to five times a week. Any form of aerobic activity, things like walking, running, biking, swimming, or hiking will work. The goal is to increase the heart rate, not get a good burn or have sweat dripping off your nose. Physical activity has many positive impacts on sleep and the way you cope with stress. Try to squeeze in some kind of exercise wherever you can—take the stairs, walk the dog, jog or bike with your kids, use a standing desk . . .

3. **Sleep.** Sleep patterns are important to your ability to cope with life and one of the most important parts of self-care. You need a minimum of six hours a night to help restore your mind and body, recharging you for the next day.

4. **Slow down, pause, stop.** Explore mindfulness, relaxation, and meditation. Learn to pause and take deep breaths; then bring your thoughts back to the present moment. Consider using apps like Calm or Headspace to help learn mindfulness and meditation. These apps can also help you learn how to breathe and relax.

5. **Take breaks from electronic media.** Put limits on screen exposure to avoid feeling overwhelmed. Sometimes you need to take a break from TV and Internet news along with social media. It is hard to care for your mind and spirit if you are constantly hit with a screen and all the noise of the media. Take some

time to unplug and focus on things that are uplifting and soothing. Spend time with nature and Scripture. The Psalms have been very helpful to me.

6. **Be kind to yourself.** There is a lot you can't control, but the one thing you can control is yourself. Learn to pay attention to your feelings and practice self-compassion. Give yourself a little grace, remembering what you have already come through and the ways God has been with you. Even people who don't struggle with anxiety can experience more worry and anxiety when stress and trauma come into their lives. So learn to practice self-compassion, and don't be too hard on and judgmental of yourself, especially if you're experiencing more anxiety than usual. Try to be curious and nonjudgmental with whatever shows up as you consider what you are feeling and what you may need at the moment.

7. **Use your supports.** When we are stressed and overwhelmed, we tend to isolate. That is the opposite of what you need. Connect to your support network. Connect to your faith community. Don't isolate. Let others know how you are doing. Ask for emotional and practical support when you need it. Consider a professional counselor to have your thoughts and feelings heard.

My professional world is that of a counselor. I sit with people hour by hour hearing distress, chaos, and hurt, but in all that, I still see the hidden beauty of each life. Each one of us possesses a beauty and strength that God places within us. I have seen how prolonged stress, conflict, and hardship can make us question whether we still have beauty, strength, or hope in our lives. I am praying you can find these from the stillness and activity of self-care.

One of the most fascinating things that comes from spending time with others is seeing what Paul in Colossians calls "Christ in you, the hope of glory" (1:27 KJV). Interacting with hurting people, seeing their strength and beauty, makes me long for Christ, His goodness, love, and kindness. In short, it gives me hope and a confident expectation that in the midst of our struggles, God is still with us. The most consistent promise in Scripture is that God is with us. My wish for you is that through this journey you see the hope, strength, and beauty God has placed within you. Part of me wishes I could sit down with each of you to hear your stories and guide you through the skills and understanding that can help your lives become healthier and fuller. That is how this book came into being. I wanted to create a guide that could help you find direction. My hope is that as you find skills to apply to your story, this book will help you find more peace, joy, and especially hope.

> My ears are filled with the sounds of promise:
> ""Good people will prosper like palm trees,
> Grow tall like Lebanon cedars;
> transplanted to God"s courtyard,
> They"ll grow tall in the presence of God,
> lithe and green, virile still in old age.""
> — PSALM 92:12–14

Chapter 2 →

The Big Four

Oh yes, you shaped me first inside, then out;
   you formed me in my mother's womb.
I thank you, High God—you're breathtaking!
   Body and soul, I am marvelously made!
   I worship in adoration—what a creation!
You know me inside and out,
   you know every bone in my body;
You know exactly how I was made, bit by bit,
   how I was sculpted from nothing into something.
Like an open book, you watched me grow from conception
to birth;
   all the stages of my life were spread out before you,
The days of my life all prepared
   before I'd even lived one day.

                              — PSALM 139:13–16

Let's imagine that I am your counselor. The Big Four—sleep, exercise, nutrition, and recreation—can help put life into perspective and provide confidence to begin working on the issues that brought you to counseling. It doesn't really matter what problem you come in with—depression, anxiety disorders, personality disorders, marital problems, grief, anger, addictions, or an inability to manage your personal or professional life. If you conquer these four areas, you have what it takes to put the problem areas of your life in order.

I can't say enough about the Big Four. The way your life functions in these four areas helps me, as your counselor, gauge the severity of your problem. Let's say I send you home after a session with the goal of making small, incremental improvements in these areas. If after two weeks you report successes, even if they are small, it's clear that your problems are not all-consuming. If you return after two weeks and report no improvement in these areas, we will know to point our therapeutic approach in another direction.

If you've ever stayed up late watching television, you know that most regularly aired programs fall by the wayside after two in the morning, often replaced with channel after channel of infomercials. Therapeutic pillows, weight-loss shakes, pills to improve libido, fitness machines, aerobic videos, and dietary supplements are but a few of the advertised products. As diverse as these products are, they all insinuate one thing— the possibility of a healthier, more enjoyable, more self-empowered life.

With so many options available for better living, you'd think humanity would struggle less. For most people, however, satisfaction remains elusive because the problems are just as numerous, unique, and unusual as the plethora of products on the market. Therapeutic pillows claim to align your spine, allowing a better night's sleep. Diet pills promote improved self-esteem and enhanced performance by helping you shed pounds. Fitness-machine ads lead to fantasies about having a chiseled body like those of the models on the screen, and dietary supplements make claims of just about every kind.

With so many options, who could blame you for feeling overwhelmed and insecure when it comes to purchasing what you need? If you take a closer look, however, you'll notice that most of these products make promises that fall into one or more of the Big Four: sleep, exercise, nutrition, and recreation.

What's Special about the Big Four

The Big Four are unique, distinguished as "outer-work"—physical actions and activities that improve how you function, both bodily and mentally. Other activities of self-care are better described as "inner-work"—practices intended to improve how you think and stimulate mental stability. The Big Four are the starting points of self-care. They are behaviors that provide a foundation from which to build. Certain inner-work methods like affirmation, mindfulness, or journaling may seem a bit foreign or something with which you are uncomfortable. If so, that's fine. Begin with the Big Four, keep an open mind, and build from there.

1. Sleep

A recent survey found that 75 percent of people sleep less than six hours per night and also experience sleep difficulties multiple nights per week. This likely comes as no surprise to you. Chances are you're one of the countless folks who toss and turn until your alarm clock blares its unwelcome racket. Normal nightly restlessness can grow out of control and bring about even bigger concerns regarding the numerous health risks associated with prolonged sleep loss:

> **Cardiovascular health.** Long-term lack of sleep can lead to hypertension, increased stress hormone levels, high blood pressure, and an irregular heartbeat.

Disease. Sleep deprivation alters immune function, increasing your chance of illness.

Brain health. Sleep helps the brain process and the commitment of important information to memory.

Metabolism and weight. Not sleeping can affect the way your body processes and stores carbohydrates. Also, your appetite can be affected by shifting hormone levels—all of which can result in unwanted weight gain.

Mood: Lack of sleep can lead to irritability, impatience, moodiness, and inability to concentrate. This can also greatly affect what you do with your free time, making you too tired to enjoy the things you love to do for recreation (Harvard Health Publications 2006).

Most of us are familiar with health risks associated with losing sleep, but have you ever considered the flip side? In most cases, a side effect of restlessness, things like thoughts during the day from stress, trauma, and memories from the past, can also be the reason you're losing sleep in the first place. The most obvious example is mood. If you toss and turn all night, your state of mind will likely sour the next day. But chances are you're fighting sleep because you're upset by memories of something that happened in the past. As the night drags on while you stare at the ceiling, your mood grows worse, frustrated by the fact you are still awake.

Perhaps you resist sleep because of fears about your health. But have you ever considered that your troubled mind and its resulting restlessness might cause your body to deteriorate much faster than it would if it were rested? Worries about health become a greater threat as frustration raises your blood pressure, causes your heart to flutter, and decreases immune and cardiovascular functions.

A vicious cycle begins. You grow to dread bedtime. You find yourself in a nightly struggle to fall asleep and stay asleep. You force yourself out of bed in the morning feeling even worse than when you attempted slumber. The cycle repeats.

How to fall asleep. A recent national survey of a thousand working adults found that nearly 25 percent admitted to often doing tasks related to their jobs in the final sixty minutes before heading to sleep (National Sleep Foundation 2008). If you're having difficulty falling asleep, you should know that working right up until the moment you slip into bed, or even while you're in bed, is one of the worst things you can do. The same can be said if you're a student or parent.

You can improve your ability to fall asleep by working to develop a nighttime ritual. In much the same way as you would get a young child ready for bed, develop steps for your body to memorize as clues that you're unwinding for the day. For example, about an hour before bed, take a warm bath; then put on cozy pajamas, and curl up on your sofa or in your bed with a good book and a cup of chamomile tea. Over time your body will become trained to respond to these actions, just as a newborn learns that after bath time, a bottle, and a few minutes being rocked, it's bedtime. If you wish to designate time to sleep, it's important you also designate time to unwind—calming your mind and warming your body.

Once you've prepared yourself for bed, your final step is to ready your bedroom by removing all distractions. Perhaps you watch TV or browse on your laptop or cell phone to induce drowsiness. Instead, try turning off electronic devices. Such mental stimuli may actually be contributing to your sleeplessness. Make an intentional effort to shake off your cares and distractions before going to bed. Make your bedroom your sanctuary of slumber.

Staying asleep. On nights when you fight tooth and nail to fall asleep, there's nothing more frustrating than finally drifting into slumber only to abruptly snap back to wakefulness in a panic. Your thoughts pick up right where they left off, and tension returns to your body. Unless you have experienced a physical injury that currently causes you pain, you may find most of the problems that hinder sleep are all in your head. It is the complicated things in life that keep you awake—looming unemployment, rocky relationships, debt, the death of a loved one, or an unpleasant desire for things to be different than they are. Your body wants to sleep, but your brain won't shut off long enough to let it rest. One way to combat complicated thoughts is to fixate your mind on mundane things.

This is why people count sheep. There's nothing special about sheep, but there is something about the exercise that works well to induce boredom. Imagining a never-ending series of identical sheep jumping over a fence and counting each one as it passes occupies your mind with simplicity, repetition, and rhythm—all things that help lull you to sleep. Perhaps you can develop your own mundane ritual. Some people count backward from one thousand, or they imagine they're mowing the lawn, passing back and forth, back and forth, slipping into slumber with each imaginary blade of grass passing underfoot. Focusing on the mundane allows your body to relax and helps you fall into sleep instead of staying keyed up with things you can't change or let go.

There's no right or wrong way to fantasize about boring things. Experiment until you find something that works for you, and as you practice the mundane, stay relaxed.

Some sleep problems can be attributed to medical conditions like thyroid problems. If the problem does not go away after trying other sleep methods, you may want to contact your physician (Vandyck et al. 1989).

2. Exercise

So far you've learned the importance of being an active participant with your life. One effective way to do so is to be physically active. Extensive studies have revealed a great deal about the benefits of regular, moderate exercise. You may be surprised by how closely mental and physical discipline are connected. The goal is to become physically, mentally, and spiritually healthier.

How exercise helps self-care. It's hard to believe, but recent reports say prescriptions of antidepressants have increased 400 percent since 1988. One out of every ten people over the age of twelve now takes some kind medication for depression (Pratt, Brody, and Gu 2011). Unfortunately, in many cases such medications are the only mental health care people ever receive. Over the past couple of generations, pills have been handed out like candy. If you suffer from severe depression, medication is likely your best way to progress toward mental stability. But if you suffer from mild or moderate depression, it may be worth exploring another, more natural and time-tested method rather than—or in addition to—antidepressants.

You may be surprised to learn that clinical trials have shown exercise to rival antidepressants in the treatment of depression, each showing the same rate of improvement. In some cases the effectiveness of exercise surpasses the effectiveness of antidepressants (Miller 2011). These results are being embraced by a growing number of mental health professionals and physicians who now encourage exercise in treating people with anxiety, depression, and eating disorders. For example,

- Studies have shown that ten months of consistent, moderate exercise out- performed some leading antidepressants in reducing symptoms of major depressive disorder.

- Studies have shown that thirty-minute workouts done three times a week cut symptoms of depression by 50 percent in young adults.

- Daily thirty-minute walks have been seen to reduce symptoms even faster than some leading antidepressants, especially in older adults (Seligson 2010).

The benefits are clear, the side effects are fewer, and both exercise and antidepressants stimulate the body to alleviate depression in much the same way. Here's how:

- Both antidepressants and exercise increase chemicals in your brain called neurotransmitters, specifically norepinephrine, serotonin, and dopamine. In fact, research indicates that the very root of depression comes from insufficient amounts of norepinephrine and serotonin, or an imbalance between these two types of neurotransmitters.

- Both antidepressants and exercise improve neurochemistry by promoting neurogenesis (the birth of new brain cells) (He et al. 2012).

It is imperative that you talk with your counselor and physician about any new physical activities or exercise programs to find a safe routine that works to enhance your physical health and stimulate an improved outlook on life. Also, don't assume exercise is the only treatment you require. Be candid with your doctor about whether you're a candidate for antidepressants if you're not already on them. If you are currently taking medication for depression, do not make any changes without the direction of your physician and mental health professional.

How exercise helps decrease anxiety. All dog owners have experienced a similar scenario: You come home after a long, hard day at work. Your feet are throbbing, and your mind is set on one goal—kicking back and relaxing. You slide your key into your front door lock, but something doesn't seem quite right. Usually your dog comes running to the sound of your jingling keys, but not this time. The house is quiet. You shudder as you anticipate what is on the other side of the door. You crack open the door and peek in. Your assumptions were correct: chewed up shoes and couch cushions are spread about the living room floor, tiny shreds of toilet paper and soggy bits that used to be the cardboard tube are scattered all over, and your dog is nowhere to be seen. Why is he hiding? Because he knows he's in deep trouble. As you gaze across the room in disapproval, you can almost imagine what must have been going through your dog's mind as he was doing this. He knew this destruction was unacceptable, proven by the fact that he's hiding. But he still couldn't help himself. Why? His acting out was the result of anxiety.

Anxiety leads to an excess of nervous energy that must be released. In fact, it *will* be released one way or another. But when this energy builds up faster than the body can release it, your state of mind becomes toxic. Imagine your body expelling nervous energy like it flushes out waste of any kind. Dead cells are discharged after blood is filtered through the kidneys. In much the same way, your body ousts anxious energy by fidgeting and increasing your heart rate and blood pressure. When you become extremely upset, you may release the surplus by crying, trembling, having an increased respiratory rate, hyperventilating, undergoing panic attacks, or acting on mood swings. The problem is that your innate physical responses are often not enough, and they only build up the tension and anxiety.

If your dog is acting out by chewing on furniture or being aggressive, the first thing an obedience trainer will tell you is to take Fido for a walk or put him on a treadmill every day because the trainer knows your dog needs to expel energy. And he will any way he can—better at a dog park than in your living room while you're away. "Man's best friends" aren't much different from their masters in this regard. If a dog is cooped up, eventually it will act out. In the same way, keeping yourself cooped up physically and emotionally will lead to negative behaviors, painful bodily tension, and poor decision making.

In times of mental unrest or physical tension, you may need to aid your body in its attempt to purge nervous waste. Walking, aerobics, stretching, weight training, basketball, dancing—it doesn't matter. Find a physical activity you enjoy and turn to it anytime you notice nervous excess. You don't need a gym to exercise. When anxiety and tension surface, find a private place to do jumping jacks or pushups or run in place—anything to increase your heart and respiratory rates, burn calories, and bring your body and mind to a relaxed state. The point is to move. Be active. It's definitely worth a shot because it just might improve how you feel and think.

Make sure you talk to your counselor and physician to confirm if you're fit to participate in any new physical activities.

3. Nutrition

In the 1970s and 1980s studies documented nutritional therapies for the treatment of mental disorders, although many were discontinued due to lack of funding. In the decades since, nutritional therapies have been pushed aside as pharmaceutical companies directed more of their attention and money to investigating synthetic drugs they could patent and sell. Consumer interest, however, has shifted over the past few years toward seeking more natural and holistic therapies. Due to the demand, nutritional therapy is once again growing in acceptance with mental health professionals, supported by a resurgence of clinical studies on the positive effects of improved diet and dietary supplements.

A proper diagnosis and treatment plan should be the first tactic when regarding mental disorders, although you need to be proactive about the type of therapy you wish to receive. Perhaps synthetic medication is your preference. If not, nutritional therapy may be a better fit for your lifestyle—as long as your counselor and physician concur.

Studies have shown that deficiencies of essential vitamins, minerals, amino acids, and omega-3 fatty acids can contribute to mental disorders (Sathyanarayana Rao et al. 2008). In many cases simply adding daily supplements and eating better may effectively reduce symptoms. Based on emerging scientific evidence, this type of holistic therapy may be appropriate for controlling a number of disorders, including major depression, anxiety disorders, bipolar disorder, schizophrenia, eating disorders, addiction, attention deficit disorder, and attention deficit hyperactivity disorder.

Consider these facts:

- Researchers have observed an increase in mental health disorders in connection with a deterioration of the Western diet.

- Studies show that populations with high fish consumption (a diet high in omega-3 fatty acid intake) have a low frequency of mental disorders.

- The most common nutritional deficiencies that contribute to mental disorders are omega-3 fatty acids, B vitamins, minerals, and amino acids that are foundations of the neurotransmitters norepinephrine, serotonin, and dopamine.

- Omega-3 fatty acids, B vitamins, and magnesium deficiencies have been linked to depression (Lakhan and Vieira 2008).

Some commonsense things. Since your early years in elementary school you've been taught to eat a balanced, healthy diet. You know that processed foods are bad for you . . . you shouldn't turn to food for comfort from stress . . . you shouldn't overeat . . . too much caffeine is bad for you . . . you should eat a healthy breakfast every day . . . chicken and fish are better for you than red meat . . . you shouldn't eat fast food every meal . . . and so on.

The point of this section on nutrition is not to develop dietary or nutritional plans but simply to educate and hopefully encourage you to consider how you eat. Let your mental health professional, physician, or nutritionist set up a nutritional plan that's tailor made for what you're going through. Do not begin any new diets or take any supplements without consulting with professionals first. But on the flip side, eating better is never a bad idea. Making good decisions about what you put into your body could mentally and physically enhance your life for years to come.

4. Recreation

Recreation—defined as a pastime, diversion, or exercise affording relaxation and enjoyment—is an essential element of the human experience and can be just about any activity. Everyone has something he or she loves to do, something in which time and problems seem to stand still. The downside for most people is a lack of hours in the day to do enjoyable things. This is a travesty, considering how important recreation is to mental and physical well-being, even if only a little "me time" two or three times a week.

Pause for a second. What is your favorite hobby or pastime? What do you do to cast your cares aside temporarily? What makes you laugh or smile? What makes time seem to stand still? Whatever it is, keep it in mind as you progress through the rest of the chapter. Maybe you were reminded of something fun you did when you were younger and are considering picking it back up. If you just now realized you actually have no recreational activity of choice, it's time to consider exploring options. Perhaps the next few pages will bring something to mind.

Laughter really is the best medicine. You've certainly heard the adage "Laughter is the best medicine." This saying has been around for ages, long before the medical community began taking interest in the actual healing power of a good time. In fact, the Bible says, "A joyful heart is good medicine" (Proverbs 17:22 NASB). People have always understood that laughter is a cure-all—lightening burdens, inspiring hope, and bringing together people of all types with its universal language—but now medical science can show us why.

Laughter significantly decreases stress levels and stimulates dopamine—a neurotransmitter known as the "feel-good chemical." It reduces depression and improves memory and motor control.

> Laughter strengthens your immune system, boosts energy, diminishes pain, and protects you from the harmful effects associated with long-term stress.

> Boisterous laughter relieves tension in your body, relaxing muscles for up to forty-five minutes afterward.

> Laughter activates the release of endorphins that promote a general sense of well-being.

> Laughter increases blood flow and the proficiency of blood vessels (Smith, Kemp, and Segal 2012).

With so much power to heal, a sense of humor and the ability to laugh are tremendously advantageous during troubling times. You can easily forget this when life comes down strong enough to drive you to counseling. As difficult as it is to believe at times, you have to know that laughter is your birthright—perhaps the most innate gift of life. Most newborns begin smiling and laughing as soon as six short weeks outside the womb. It's something you are born to do and intended to continue throughout your days. Even in the most difficult times, simple moments when you let go of pain and laugh a little can go a long way, allowing you to see your condition more clearly in a less threatening light.

When laughter is hard to come by. Seek it out. Watch a funny movie or television show, preferably with at least one friend or loved one. Laughter is contagious and easier to get lost in with other people around. Examples of group activities would be visiting a comedy club, hosting a game night, going to a karaoke club, participating in team sports, and playing with children. You may need to set aside time and energy to seek out a good time, even if it seems like a chore at first. It's like anything else: it takes work to see results. It may be hard initially, but diligently pursuing opportunities to laugh is a key to improving your outlook on life. Eventually, with practice, enjoyment will become second nature, incorporated into the very fabric of your life.

How hobbies help. "What would you do if you had a million dollars?" is a common question asked by school counselors every day, but it's also a great way to find out your hobby of choice. By definition, a hobby is something you do for enjoyment that isn't what you do for a living. It's an enjoyable activity you would do all the time to stimulate your mind, body, or both if money were taken out of the equation.

As you've already learned and will continually be reminded in this book, a healthy mind depends on a healthy body and vice versa. It's a balancing act. Some hobbies cross over into exercise, which we looked at earlier in the chapter. Other hobbies add a different take on the word *exercise.* Just as physical activities keep your body strong and limber, mental activities—those that require problem-solving and memory recall—keep your mind sharp and agile. Without something to encourage mental stimulation, your brain can atrophy, as would muscles that get little use. This can lead to a fall in cognitive function regardless of age. Such mental exercises include

- Working puzzles

- Traveling

- Reading books and writing

- Playing cards, checkers, chess, crossword puzzles, bingo, board games like Scrabble, and other games that require thought

- Collecting stamps or coins

- Restoring old cars and antiques

- Woodworking and metalworking

- Doing crafts like painting, drawing, or ceramics

If you love doing something, chances are someone else loves it too. Why not seek out like-minded people who share your passion? Adding social interaction to a hobby is a double bonus for both the mind and body and increases your odds of enjoying the positive effects of laughing with others. In fact, studies have linked strong, regular social ties to lower blood pressure and longer life expectancy, as well as boosting cognitive functioning, memory, and intellectual performance (Uchino, Uno, and Holt-Lunstad 1999). This just goes to show that people are good medicine too.

Just because sleep, exercise, nutrition, and recreation are lumped together as the Big Four, they don't need to be treated as one overarching homework assignment. Instead, treat each one individually—the Big Four broken up into "four smaller ones"—and don't be afraid to take baby steps. Pick one activity you can currently take on, and actively work on it with the help of your counselor. As you gain ground in one area, others are bound to fall in line. There are many things you can do to improve mental health and reduce stress, but the biggest bang for the buck is going to come from the Big Four.

Chapter 3

Relaxation:
How to Let Go

Do not be anxious about anything, but in everything by prayer and supplication with thanksgiving let your requests be made known to God.

> — PHILIPPIANS 4:6 ESV

The Lord is my shepherd; I shall not want.
　He makes me lie down in green pastures.
He leads me beside still waters.
　He restores my soul.
He leads me in paths of righteousness
　for his name's sake.

> — PSALM 23:1–3 ESV

We relax in the grand beauty of God's perfect promises.

> — ANDREW FARLEY

Of all the things we ask you to do in this book, you may enjoy this assignment the most. Let's face it: relaxation feels better than tension. In this chapter, instead of asking you to do more, we ask you to do less, to take it easy, to let go, to release. When you do this you'll find that your neck and shoulders unwind, your teeth do not grind, and your headaches subside quickly or even immediately.

For most of us, our body and thoughts are on autopilot. We don't consciously recognize how tense and stressed our bodies are. This chapter teaches awareness and skills to help you care for your body.

For me, both my mind and body felt like tangled, twisted, and taut messes when I began learning relaxation. My head and neck hurt constantly. I remember my legs, especially my calf muscles, aching, and I found it hard even to walk at times. My mind was so full of painful and regretful thoughts I couldn't think straight. It was as though there were no room left for any goodness to develop.

Learning to relax may have been the most beneficial part of self-care for me. My counselor taught me some basic relaxation and breathing exercises that I use to this day. He taught me how to do them while sitting, lying down, and even standing. He also explained the health risks involved with staying so stressed. Luckily, the process of unwinding took place before any long-term damage was done.

The Importance of Relaxation

Perhaps you're wondering why something as seemingly simple as relaxation merits its own chapter. If you take a moment to turn your attention to your body, you'll find the answer. Before reading further, notice how tense your shoulders are. If the tightness isn't immediately apparent, take one long, deep breath, and as you exhale, allow the tops of your shoulders to drop and your arms to go limp.

Did you feel the difference? Repeat this several more times. It's surprising how much deeper you fall into rest each time your breath releases.

Next, notice your face. Chances are your forehead is slightly scrunched, your teeth are clenched, or your eyes are squinted. Relax the muscles in your face as if they're melting or drooping toward the floor. This simple exercise displays but a glimpse of the rigid state your body holds every waking moment.

Think about how you carry yourself throughout the day. Are you one of the countless people who suck your stomach in while in public to appear thinner? Do you broaden your shoulders to appear brawnier? Does your posture create tension in your neck, back, and shoulders? If you think relaxation is something that comes easily, you're about to learn how elusive it can actually be.

Relaxation gets its own chapter for several reasons.

1. Staying relaxed physically is crucial to mental health.

2. Staying relaxed mentally is crucial to physical health.

3. Most people don't realize how tense they are.

4. Most people don't know how to relax, much less remain in a relaxed state.

The Mind-Body Connection

Mind and body are connected more than we realize. Think about something you're afraid of—whether it's snakes, spiders, heights, or whatever else the case may be—and your body will no doubt respond with a cringe, shivers, or goose bumps. The same goes for recalling trauma. Reliving the memory of a car wreck can cause your body to reenact, to a lesser degree, the physical strain that occurred during the accident. In much the same way, harboring bodily tension preserves traumatic memories as your body reminds your brain of the physical stress you endured. Mind and body go hand in hand. A tense body leads to racing thoughts, and racing thoughts lead to a tense body. Similarly, a relaxed body leads to a relaxed mind, just as a relaxed mind leads to a body at ease.

The Balancing Act

Tranquility isn't something attained only in a hammock, on a beach, or in a fishing boat. Likewise, relaxation won't be found solely in excessive fantasies of exotic destinations. Such reverie alone will only lead to feelings of longing for something out of reach. For genuine relaxation to take hold, your mind and body must work together instead of against each other.

At some point you've probably said while preparing to head home from a vacation, "Oh, well. Time to go back to the real world." But it's incorrect to assume your vacation was somehow less real. Digging your toes into the sand while sipping an icy drink is just as real as when you punch the time clock, argue with your spouse, or sit across from your counselor. No matter where you are—whether on vacation or in "the real world"—your mind is capable of stressing you out and hindering relaxation. Physically you're always vulnerable, as trouble will follow you wherever you go. If you're a parent, you know you can argue with your children just as fervently on a trip as you do at home, leaving you in need of a vacation from your vacation.

Perhaps you know what it's like struggling to relax on a sandy beach because of thoughts about your job and the stresses awaiting you at the office. Or perhaps you have experienced the anguish of joining your family for a photo on the beach. You pull your loved ones close and point a fake smile to the camera, knowing your marriage is failing, and you wonder if this will be the last picture of you all together. This goes to show that hell on earth can find you wherever you are, even vacationing in paradise.

You don't need a hot tub to relax and be content. You don't have to be in a pool to enjoy your children. You don't have to walk hand in hand on the shore with your wife to show her affection, and you don't have to go into debt for a vacation you can't afford to get away from the cares of the world. It's time to throw away phony notions of how to relax and to understand that you can reach a deep level of rest at any given moment, a state stronger than you have ever experienced by simply balancing your mind and body.

Relaxation Techniques

Numerous relaxation techniques exist. Counselors will usually have a few tips up their sleeves just for their clients. There are also several good apps that will give you guided relaxation. A counselor can often notice your anxiety in a session and may offer to lead you through an exercise. Likewise, if you feel that stress or tension prevent you from engaging completely in a session, ask your counselor for an appropriate relaxation intervention to meet your needs.

Some relaxation techniques require professional guidance, but many don't. Plenty of do-it-yourself methods allow you to achieve tranquility yourself. Remember: you are the expert of your own life, and it's up to you to explore what works for your particular tension. To help you get started, the remainder of this section contains self-help techniques to increase serenity by balancing your mind and body.

Deep-breathing exercise. Stress typically affects your breathing, resulting in short, shallow, and erratic breaths, while calm is associated with deep, long, and balanced inhalations and exhalations. Practicing deep breathing is simple and can be done just about anywhere, anytime. When you notice stress in your breathing,

- Inhale once deeply, completely filling your lungs.

- Let out a large sigh, dropping your chest and shoulders, pushing the air out through pursed lips and completely emptying your lungs. This action will help snap you out of your current agitated mental and physical state.

- Next, begin breathing deeply. Imagine your belly and the area around your waistline as a deep, powerful place.

- Focus your concentration on the feeling of your breath flowing in and out.

- When you inhale, feel your entire abdomen, sides, and lower back expand.

- Notice the subtle pause that occurs just before you exhale.

- When you exhale, focus on the sensations that come as your abdomen, sides, and lower back return to a resting position.

- Notice the subtle pause that occurs just before you inhale again.

- Repeat this cycle ten times, relaxing your chest and shoulders more fully each time, eventually including your neck, face, and arm muscles.

This exercise offers a perfect example of how you can achieve balance by leading with your body. Focusing attention on the rhythm of bodily movements that occur during breathing naturally directs your mind away from your stressor and incites your mind to join up with the body, allowing mind and body to transition together into rest.

Progressive muscle relaxation. This is a two-step process. It involves systematically constricting and relaxing specific muscles groups. Here is a typical way to practice:

- Sit or lie down and get comfortable.

- Take a few moments to relax and breathe deeply.

- When you feel ready, direct your attention to your right foot and focus for a few moments on how it feels.

- Slowly tense the muscles in that foot as tightly as you can and hold for a count of ten.

- Completely release the tension in your foot, and focus solely on the tension clearing and how the foot feels once it is completely limp.

- When you're ready, shift your focus to the left foot, and repeat the sequence of tension and release.

- Continue this way through the entire body. A typical pattern is (1) right foot, (2) left foot, (3) right calf, (4) left calf, (5) right thigh, (6) left thigh, (7) hips and buttocks, (8) abdomen, (9) chest, (10) back, (11) right arm, (12) left arm, (13) right hand, (14) left hand, (15) neck and shoulders, and (16) face.

With consistent practice, progressive muscle relaxation reveals the countless sensations you experience on the continuum between extreme tension and total rest. You will also develop an intimate awareness of where and how you hold tension. This understanding will help you notice and reduce the early signs of muscular tension that accompany stress. And just as with deep breathing, the body takes the lead with the intent of the mind joining it in deep rest.

Consult with your physician before practicing progressive muscle relaxation if you have a history of muscle spasms, back problems, or other injuries that may be heightened by constricting muscles.

Mindfulness meditation. You may be one of the many people who think meditation is something reserved for gurus, Eastern religions, New Agers, or believers of pseudoscience. You may think that meditation involves twisting your legs in uncomfortable positions and sitting motionless for hours on end, chanting "oohs" and "ohms" or even praying to a deity. With mindfulness meditation, all these assumptions are incorrect. We will examine mindfulness more fully in the next chapter, but we also mention it here because of one of the benefits associated with meditation—deep relaxation.

You may be wondering what mindfulness meditation is. Let us answer this by breaking the phrase in two: *mindfulness* and *meditation*. *Mindfulness* can be defined as purposely and nonjudgmentally paying attention in the present moment. Essentially, mindfulness is about developing awareness of the present—living fully engaged in each passing moment, accepting things exactly as they are with less criticism. Defining *meditation* is a little more complicated because different types exist, many intended to achieve different goals. All forms of mindfulness meditation, however, have one central goal—to foster present-moment awareness. If it is helpful, think of mindfulness as a byproduct of meditation and meditation as a way to generate mindfulness in all areas of your life. Some would even say that any activity that helps you focus on what is happening in the moment—whether in your surroundings or within yourself—could be considered a form of meditation. For you, this may be knitting, swimming, painting, jogging, folding laundry, or washing dishes.

Washing dishes is a wonderful example of how to meditate on something usually considered mundane or bothersome. Next time you do them, step out of your mind, away from the stressful thoughts that haunted your day, and focus instead on the warmth of the water, the smell of the soap, the sound of the dishes clanging against each other, and the sight of flowing water cascading off each dish as you rinse. If you look closely, you may even notice your reflection replicated hundreds of times in each of the tiny bubbles formed by the detergent.

The goal of mindfulness meditation is not to produce a trance-like state in which no thinking occurs. Rather, the goal is to pay attention to what is happening—whatever that may be. It may be a sensation in a particular body part like pleasure, pain, numbness, or tingling. It may be an emotional feeling like happiness, sorrow, shame, or boredom. It may be drowsiness or anxiety. Or you may pay attention to thoughts that are on your mind. Many of us never relax because we are not aware that we are not relaxed. In a sense, we never pay attention to the fact that we never pay attention, and so we never notice our mind-body imbalance. Mindfulness meditation is important for relaxation because of its amazing ability to balance the body and mind simply by paying attention to the imbalance.

We'll look at other methods of meditation in the next chapter, but here we will discuss one type—the body scan—because of its relaxing qualities. In this particular meditation the mind takes the lead by focusing intensely on the body.

You will notice that the body scan is similar in practice to progressive muscle relaxation in that you focus attention on one body part at a time. In the body scan, however, you neither tense nor relax your muscles. You don't try to create any kind of state in your body at all. Instead, you simply observe the body. This concentration soothes the mind and in turn brings a natural tranquility to the body. Here is how to practice the body scan:

- Lie flat on your back or sit up straight in a chair. Your eyes can be open or closed, whichever seems more appropriate. Allow your arms and legs to fall loosely.

- Focus on your breathing at the point of your nostrils or the rising and falling of your abdomen for a couple of minutes or until you feel some of your immediate tension melt away.

- Turn your full attention to the toes on your left foot. Notice any sensations. These could include sensations formed by contact with your socks, or blanket if you are covered up. Feel your toes touching each other. This may create a tingling sensation. If you feel pain or numbness, don't resist the feeling. Simply observe it just as it is.

- As you inhale, imagine your breath traveling from your nose all the way down to your toes, and then imagine the air flowing back up and out the nose with each exhale. Keep your focus on the toes in this way for one to two minutes.

- If your mind wanders and you lose concentration on the body, that's perfectly fine. Just noticing that you were not aware brings instant awareness. All you have to do is bring your attention back to the particular body part and resume concentration. If you lose focus a hundred times, gently and without judgment bring your attention back to the body a hundred times.

- Next move to the rest of the foot and offer it the same undivided attention.

- Continue this routine of concentration and breathing into each body part. A typical pattern is (1) left toes, (2) left foot, (3) left ankle, (4) left calf, (5) left shin, (6) left knee, (7) left thigh, (8) right toes, (9) right foot, (10) right ankle, (11) right calf, (12) right shin, (13) right knee, (14) right thigh, (15) hips and buttocks, (16) abdomen, (17) chest, (18) back, (19) left arm, (20) left hand, (21) left fingers, (22) right arm, (23) right hand, (24) right fingers, (25) neck, shoulders, and throat, (26) top of head, and (27) face.

- Once awareness has been brought to the face, draw your attention to your nostrils and focus on the sensations that occur from the act of breathing.

- After a few moments, direct your attention to the abundance of sensations occurring throughout the body.

- When you are ready, conclude by opening your eyes slowly and expanding your awareness to the room around you.

We recommend that you use an audio recording if you are new to the practice.

One final note on mindfulness. Take time throughout each day to snap out of your mind and pay attention to what your body is saying in each moment. Where are you tense? Where are you relaxed? Are there times during the day when tension is at its highest point? Are there places you frequent that cause you to tense more than others? If so, you may be able to develop relaxation methods to prepare you before entering these specific times and places. This will allow you to approach stress with more tranquility and confidence and less insecurity and desperation. Are there times during the day when you feel at ease and exceptionally relaxed? If so, perhaps you can adjust your schedule to make more time for these things. Investigating and answering these questions are important steps to understanding more about yourself and what you need to take better care of yourself.

Visualization. Visualization, or guided imagery, is a type of meditation that differs from mindfulness. Instead of accepting and bringing awareness to stressful situations, visualization employs fantasy to foster tranquility. When used as a relaxation technique, visualization involves imagining a peaceful scene in which you can feel comfortable letting go of tension and anxiety. The choice of scenery is up to you. Perhaps it is a tropical beach, a spot enjoyed during childhood, a favorite fishing hole, or a field with long, flowing grass. You may choose to do this exercise in silence or while listening to relaxing music, your counselor's guiding voice during a session, a recording of your counselor, or an audio recording that reflects the scene you are creating in your mind—for example, picture yourself in a forest and play a track of forest sounds.

Here is an example of how you might practice visualization of a beach scene at sunset:

- Play an audio track of crashing waves if you choose.

- Lie flat on the ground or sit up straight in a chair.

- Close your eyes and imagine as vividly as possible the beach scene. Try to create reactions from all your senses. Listen to the waves. Look at the purple and orange sky created by the setting sun and the seagulls flying overhead. Smell and taste the salty air. Feel the heavy breeze and the sand between your toes. It may be difficult for all your senses to come alive. Take one sense at a time, and see if you can create activity in at least three of them.

- Walk up and down the beach. Feel the water rush over your feet. Look for seashells. Explore what is in your imaginary place, and allow your body to fall into deep relaxation.

- When your mind drifts off, simply return to your scene, and allow your senses to again come to life.

- When you are ready, conclude by opening your eyes slowly and expanding your awareness of the room around you. Be careful that your return to reality does not cause unnecessary feelings of displeasure or longing to escape. Keep in mind that visualization is intended to release tension and anxiety, not cause more.

Massage. Oftentimes excessive tension resides in your muscles, causing aches and pains, tightness, and headaches. If you have the time and money, treating yourself on occasion to a professional massage can work wonders and leave you in a deep state of relaxation. If your wallet or schedule are just too tight, don't let that stop you from unwinding. You may be surprised at the amount of relief you can experience from simply massaging yourself. After all, you are the expert of your own body, and you know best where your problem areas reside.

Let's say you feel a tension headache forming in your neck and shoulders. First, take a moment to breathe, relax, and drop your shoulders, just as you did in the exercise at the beginning of this chapter. Once you feel some of the initial rigidity melt away, place your right palm on the right side of your neck. Likewise, place your left palm on the left side of your neck and interlock your fingers. In this position, squeeze your neck and roll your hands around, discovering and focusing on the areas that seem to need the most attention. From this same position, try pointing your thumbs straight down and using them to accurately dig into the strongest tension areas and muscle knots. You will find that your thumbs can make contact from the base of your skull to your shoulder joints. You can try placing your thumbs at the top of your neck and then slowly traveling down along the sides of the vertebrae of your neck. As you do this, focus on relaxing the neck and shoulder muscles, and visualize them loosening as your thumbs pass along them. Continue this down the neck and across the tops of the shoulders. Repeat until you feel relief.

This is just one idea and one area of the body. Remember that you are the expert, so explore where you hold tension and different ways to massage yourself. Other examples may include soaking your feet in warm water and giving yourself a foot massage at the end of a long, hard day, or rolling your fingers around your temples or forehead when a headache encroaches on your ability to work or socialize. The good news is that self-massage can be done just about anywhere, anytime.

When and Where to Relax

The exercises above are just a handful of ways to go about relaxing. The good news is there's no right or wrong way. It's something you can do anytime wherever you are. You may assume you need a quiet room, bubble bath, fishing boat, and so on, but saying you need those things is like saying you need a gym membership and a personal trainer to exercise. You don't. You just have to be creative with your commitment to calm yourself when you need it.

No matter where you are, you can always find a relaxation technique that will work for your situation. You can practice deep breathing while sitting at your desk. You can give yourself a massage while sitting in traffic. You can practice being mindful wherever you are: driving, walking, or waiting in line. No matter how or where you go about it, the key is separating yourself from anxiety and tension and focusing instead on allowing your taut mind and muscles to let go.

The Consequences of Stress

Please understand that stress shouldn't be viewed as something negative. In fact, your stress reaction is meant to protect you. Your body instinctively reacts to stressful situations, a result from the time when attacks from predators like lions and tigers were a legitimate concern for mankind. Such aggressors are rare today, but that doesn't mean there is less to worry about in our civilized age. You likely face demanding workloads, family issues, a fast-paced life, and economic turmoil. Compact these irritants with a traumatic event, and your body naturally associates your mental stress as a physical assault and responds by tensing as if you are under constant attack.

If you're startled—say you narrowly miss being hit by a car—your hypothalamus, a small region located at the base of your brain, sets off a chain of events in your body. Nerve and hormonal signals prompt your adrenal glands, located atop your kidneys, to surge hormones, including cortisol and adrenaline.

- *Cortisol* is a stress hormone that affects sugar (glucose) levels; tissue repair; the immune, digestive, and reproductive systems; growth processes; mood; motivation; and anxiety.

- *Adrenaline* increases your heart rate, elevates your blood pressure, and boosts energy supplies.

This chemical response is essential to your survival. It is the alarm system that triggers the "fight-or-flight" reaction. The problem occurs when your stress response no longer self-regulates. Sometimes it gets stuck in the *on* position, not allowing hormone levels to decrease to normal once a perceived threat has passed. This leads to chronic tension.

Long-term activation of the stress response—and the subsequent overexposure to cortisol and adrenaline—can disrupt almost every bodily process. This puts you at increased risk of numerous health problems and diseases, including

- heart disease

- acid peptic disease

- sleep problems

- asthma

- fatigue

- tension headaches

- alcoholism and drug abuse

- hypertension

- ulcers

- depression

- obesity

- irritable bowel syndrome

- psychoneuroses

- sexual dysfunction

- memory impairment

- skin conditions and diseases like psoriasis, lichen planus, urticaria, pruritus, neurodermatitis, and others (Contrada and Baum 2010)

Why Some People Handle Stress Better Than Others

Everyone reacts differently to stress and trauma. Maybe you're the laid-back type who lets everything roll off your back, or perhaps you react strongly to the slightest appearance of stress. Wherever you land on the spectrum of these two extremes, most responses to stress fall under one of two categories.

- **Life experiences.** Strong stress reactions can be traced to your early life. People who as children experienced traumatic events such as abuse or neglect tend to be particularly vulnerable to stress as adults.

- **Genetics.** Genes that govern stress response keep most people on a fairly even keel, though overactive or underactive stress responses may stem from variations in these genes.

Face-to-face time with your counselor during sessions will certainly reveal how life experiences and genetics affect your response to trauma and stress (Contrada and Baum 2010).

The Benefits of Relaxation

When trauma occurs or life becomes excessively hectic, relaxation is too often the first thing to take a back seat in your life, causing you to miss the benefits associated with a mind and body balanced and at rest. Practicing relaxation techniques on a regular basis positively affects almost every bodily system by appropriately switching your stress response to the off position, allowing your hormone levels to balance out. These benefits include

- slowing your heart rate

- lowering your blood pressure

- slowing your breathing rate

- increasing blood flow to major muscles

- reducing muscle tension and chronic pain

- improving concentration

- reducing anger and frustration

- boosting confidence to handle problems (Payne and Donaghy 2010)

To gain the most benefit, try combining elements of different techniques. For example, try adding deep breathing or mindful awareness to a self-massage. Feel free to combine relaxation techniques with homework outcomes mentioned in other chapters.

With practice you should expect to see improvement in how you carry your tension and stress. As you grow more comfortable and confident in arriving at a deep state of rest while practicing relaxation techniques, you'll carry tranquility with you after you conclude the exercises and go about your day. You'll grow more mindful of tension in your body, the nature of your thoughts, and your environment.

Relaxation is a skill that improves with practice. Initially, you may have a difficult time balancing your mind and body. Don't be discouraged by this; focusing on transitioning from states of agitation to relaxation takes a lot of energy. If a particular technique doesn't feel like a good fit, try another. If none of your attempts at relaxation work, talk to your counselor about other options. In some cases, especially if you have a history of abuse, you may experience emotional discomfort with certain relaxation techniques. Rushes of emotion during deep relaxation are common, but if they ever become unbearable, stop and talk to your counselor about what to try instead.

A word of caution: as you learn to let go through relaxation, thoughts may surface that are difficult to deal with. I've found that tense bodies often repress thoughts and feelings. True relaxation gets you in touch with the reality that your mind and body are connected, and this connection may reveal old wounds. Through years of personal work and counseling, I've learned to recognize tension that often creeps up my neck, shoulders, and jaw. These sensations act as red flags to notify me I am struggling mentally with something my body is trying to hide. Be prepared to talk with your counselor about what relaxation reveals to you, and learn to recognize tension in your own body. What is it hiding?

Chapter 4

Mindfulness:
Learning to Meditate and Live in the Present

Let the words of my mouth and the meditation of my heart be acceptable in your sight, O Lord, my rock and my redeemer.

— PSALM 19:14 ESV

I will meditate on your precepts and fix my eyes on your ways.

— PSALM 119:15 ESV

May my meditation be pleasing to him, for I rejoice in the Lord.

— PSALM 104:34 ESV

But his delight is in the law of the Lord, and on his law he meditates day and night.

— PSALM 1:2 ESV

What if you truly are who God says you are? After all, when our view of ourselves disagrees with God's view of us, who's right?

— ANDREW FARLEY

A good definition of *mindfulness* is "a process of focusing your attention on the present." The goal is to not be distracted by other thoughts constantly running through your head. The intent is to clear "noise" from your mind.

The terms *grounding* or *mindfulness* can be used interchangeably and are characterized by meditation and relaxation techniques. The purpose is to become more self-aware. You pay attention to your thoughts, feelings, and sensations in the present moment—without deciding whether they're good or bad and without becoming overwhelmed or overly reactive. The goal is to pay attention to the present moment.

As a clinical mental health counselor, I'm thoroughly impressed with the wealth of research that has been published about mindfulness. Time and time again, studies have reinforced the therapeutic value of mindfulness meditation—an ancient practice that has been used by millions of people for thousands of years. Simply put, it works.

Problems of life and mental disorders distort how you see the world. Mindfulness can realign your perspective back to the richness of the present moment rather than being misled by the wounds of the past and fears of the future. It's amazing to me that most clients don't realize they are lost in their thoughts. They blindly follow the scripts and lies of their mind. I love to empower clients by simply stating, "You can choose how to respond to thoughts. You don't have to believe everything your mind tells you." For many, this is a life-changing moment. I remember that for me, the novel thought at the time was that I get to choose what I think about. So often it feels as if we have no control over our thoughts, emotions, and will; mindfulness helps us learn we can control them.

The Bible has a lot to say about calming our minds and keeping a focus on the One who lovingly created us and knows us intimately.

- In Philippians Paul reminds us to be mindful and live with an awareness of the present (see Philippians 2:1–5).

- Prayer can be a practical way to apply mindfulness to our daily life (see 1 Thessalonians 5:17).

- In the Bible meditation can be seen as spending time studying Scripture (see Psalm 48:9 and 63:6).

- Our goal is to look to Jesus and think about true, admirable things (see Hebrews 12:2 and Philippians 4:8).

- We shouldn't let ourselves be distracted by worry about the future (see Matthew 6:25–34).

- The Bible instructs us to take every thought captive (see 2 Corinthians 10:5).

- Paul teaches us to be transformed by renewing our minds (see Romans 12:2) and to focus on God-honoring thoughts (see Philippians 4:9).

The opening of the chapter on relaxation guided you in this simple breathing exercise to offer a glimpse of tension in your body:

> Before reading further, notice how tense your shoulders are. If the tightness isn't immediately apparent, take one long, deep breath, and as you exhale, allow the tops of your shoulders to drop and your arms to go limp. Did you feel the difference?

Repeat this several more times. It's surprising how much deeper you fall into rest each time your breath releases. Next, notice your face. Chances are your forehead is slightly scrunched, your teeth are clenched, or your eyes are squinted. Relax the muscles in your face, as if they're melting or drooping toward the floor.

This exercise is handy for setting up a discussion on relaxation. It also works well to introduce the topic of this chapter, mindfulness meditation.

Mindfulness Meditation

Recall that in the previous chapter we looked at each word of the phrase *mindfulness meditation*. We defined *mindfulness* as purposely and nonjudgmentally paying attention to the present moment. Put another way, being mindful is living in the here and now. It is being attentive and aware of exactly what is happening. In the relaxation exercise above, you experienced mindfulness when you snapped out of your thoughts and instead focused your attention on your shoulders. For a split second—before judging the tension, before recalling an injury, before resisting discomfort—you experienced pure, unadulterated mindfulness.

People have used numerous methods of meditation throughout history, and many are still used today. Some are used for spiritual or religious devotion. In the evangelical Christian world, spending time with God is seen as the practice of devotions—a focused time for thoughts, words, and study. We tend to think of prayer as a time of talking to God and thinking about Scripture. Mindfulness is considered being with God in each moment, trying to pay attention in a way that creates an awareness of God's presence and all that He provides in that moment. Mindfulness can be seen as praying without ceasing. One of the goals of Christian mindfulness is learning to be with God each moment of our day. Mindfulness can be a way of watching over our heart and mind so we are not fooled by lies and inaccurate thoughts and can maintain a clear understanding and receive the good gifts each moment has to offer. It can be a way of opening ourselves authentically to God's beautiful healing presence. If it helps, think of mindfulness as a byproduct of meditation, and meditation as a way to generate mindfulness in all areas of your life.

The Opposite of Mindfulness

As a human being, you experience two states of consciousness. You just learned a little bit about one. It is the focus of this chapter—mindfulness. You encountered this state when you focused awareness on your body during the relaxation exercise. You were aware of yourself. You were attentive to the felt sensations in your body. You brought balance as you connected your mind with your body, if only for a brief moment.

Unfortunately, mindfulness is not a typical human experience. If you're like most people, you pay close attention to your body and your surroundings only during unusually beautiful or traumatic events. Instead, you spend most of your time in a state of *mindlessness*—the opposite of mindfulness. This term is not used to signify stupidity or dimwittedness. Rather, it means existing solely in your head, being led by the current of your thoughts, believing whatever your thoughts tell you, and maneuvering through life on autopilot. It is the state that prevented you from noticing the tension in your shoulders. Mindlessness is a distracting condition that inhibits you from paying attention to reality as it unfolds. Instead, you fixate on thoughts that project a mere image of reality that is usually distorted or fictional.

It's impossible to be present day to day when your mindless mind is constantly somewhere else. It's like trying to watch a movie while babysitting a dozen children—you catch only bits and pieces of the story between changing diapers, breaking up squabbles, mending scraped knees, and answering an unending stream of questions. With so many distractions, you miss crucial plot and character information. To make sense of what you're watching, you recall memories of the bits you did catch, predict what you think may have unfolded, and fantasize about different endings. This sounds frustrating and a terrible way to watch television, but it's exactly how your thoughts sidetrack most of your waking life, and you don't even know it.

Three types of thoughts contribute to mindlessness: memories of the past, predictions about the future, and fantasies. Let's take a look at how these thoughts interweave in your mind and act as smoke and mirrors to distract you from living mindfully.

Memories of the past. Memories are essential. Without them you would not be able to make decisions or interpret information about your environment. Though they have a purpose, memories can lead to a mindless state if they repeat excessively and distort over time.

Feedback loops. If you've ever been to a concert, you've certainly heard the annoying, ear-piercing sound of a microphone that's turned up too loud. It squeals and screeches while you in the crowd grumble and glare back to the sound booth for someone to fix the shrill noise before your hearing is damaged. This occurrence is caused by the microphone picking up the sound of itself not just once but countless times. It continues until it's overloaded by its own source, resulting in the ear-splitting racket known as feedback. In much the same way, condemning voices, hurtful words, and visions of traumatic instances from your past repeat over and over in your mind, fighting for your attention. They grow louder and louder until you can no longer hear yourself think. Memories can be deafening.

Memories of childhood. Your counselor may delve into your childhood. There's a reason for this. A great number of theorists agree that the childhood years are the most important to development. Much of the person you are was forged in the years leading up to adulthood. Now that you're older, all you have left of your younger years are memories—some good, some bad. The bad are usually the most aggressive, demanding to be recalled much more often and more vividly than memories of good times. In fact, if you take a moment to write down your five strongest childhood memories, don't be surprised if some are related to death, abuse, or a broken home.

1. _____

2. _____

3. _____

4. _____

5. _____

There's a problem with carrying hurtful memories into adulthood. When you were a child, you viewed pain from a childish perspective. Now that you're an adult, you have a greater understanding of how the world works. Things that cause emotional pain to a child may be little trouble for a grown-up. In this light, it may be safe to assume that many of your painful childhood memories are misinterpretations of things you simply weren't capable of understanding at the time. You've carried these troubling recollections into adulthood and attempted to rationalize them by dwelling on the past. Inability to let go of a troubled childhood is common for most people and has led to a society of grown-ups who are little more than children emotionally trapped in adult bodies, attempting to solve adult problems from childish perspectives.

Tall tales. People love tall tales. Everyone has heard an example of a hunting story of "the one that got away." Each time the tale is told the animal grows larger and the storyteller adds more points to its antlers. The brain is prone to embellishing thoughts in an effort to retain memories. If instances are made larger than life, they're easier to remember. This ensures that important events are successfully placed in long-term storage, but it does little to ensure the integrity of the story. It goes to show that what you recall as true may be a distortion of the truth or a flat-out lie.

Predictions about the future. The future has not yet happened. Many people seem to overlook this fact. People spend enormous amounts of time, energy, and money betting on the future as the sole solution to their problems. This is a recipe for disaster, considering that any number of unforeseen events could throw a wrench into even the most thought-out plans. Life's outcome is unpredictable and sometimes can seem ruthless. People spend their lives accumulating riches beyond measure only to lose them all for one reason or another. Life can strip more than just belongings or titles; friends and family are also vulnerable to its uncertainty. Anything physical (possessions and relationships) or emotional (dignity and courage) can be lost in an instant regardless of the amount of planning and safeguarding. Chances are you have recently experienced a loss or discouragement that has led you to counseling or this book.

With such uncertainty, the future is no place to hang your hat—it might not be there when the present catches up. This isn't to say you don't need to look ahead in life. You have to believe better days are ahead. Just be careful with your expectations. After all, you're dissatisfied with your current situation because things didn't work out the way you once planned or assumed they would. Let that be a lesson to you. The future can be a great source of disappointment if you arrive at your destination and don't find what you were looking for. It's good to set goals for yourself as you progress through counseling, although you should allow some breathing room for the future to develop. Don't be surprised if you grow in new and exciting ways you never would have anticipated.

Fantasies. Another problem of mindless thinking deals with frequently fantasizing about things contrary to your own circumstances. Countless times a day you imagine yourself, other people, and other things in different situations. Sometimes you'll watch mental movies of yourself on great adventures. You might imagine yourself as a superhero, astronaut, rock star, Olympic athlete, or just somebody else. Often you fantasize about something you want, which leads to a desire for things you don't have. We all think of things that are depressing, exciting, scary, disgusting, and so forth. The list goes on and on.

These musings are helpful if your intent is to be able to handle yourself better when a similar situation occurs. Still, it is a slippery slope, especially if you linger on hurtful instances. You're liable to get stuck in a past moment fantasizing about how you would return pain on the person who wronged you or imagining yourself in your villain's shoes, assuming to know the intent of the person's actions or words. This type of thinking is of no help to your healing. It will only lead to mental feedback loops and warped memories of painful instances.

Practicing Formal Mindfulness Meditation

At this point you may still feel a bit confused about what mindfulness meditation is. You've read our definitions of *mindfulness* and *meditation*, but it's still not sinking in. To be frank, it won't sink in until you try it. Meditation is one of those things that can't be accurately explained with words on a page. It's like riding a bicycle; you can instruct someone who has never ridden how to keep his balance, but that information is of no use on its own. It must be experienced. It takes time and commitment. Mistakes have to be made. You have to develop a feel for it. This is why people say they "practice" meditation. It's an ongoing experience.

Several meditative techniques are categorized as mindfulness practices. Common methods include the body scan, sitting meditation, lovingkindness meditation, walking meditation, mountain meditation, and yoga. In this chapter we will review the body scan from chapter 3 and discuss the most common method of mindfulness meditation: sitting meditation.

Descriptions of multiple mindfulness meditations are beyond the scope of this book. This chapter is merely intended to get you started.

The body scan meditation. The body scan is a technique geared toward establishing a connection with the body. It's a wonderful method for new meditators because it cultivates extended concentration and heightened awareness, both important qualities for mindfulness meditation. Here is how you practice the body scan:

- Lie flat on your back or sit up straight in a chair. Your eyes can be open or closed, whichever seems more appropriate. Allow your arms and legs to fall loosely.

- Focus on your breathing at the point of your nostrils or the rising and falling of your abdomen for several minutes.

- Turn your full attention to the toes on your left foot. Notice any sensations. These could include sensations formed by contact with your socks, or blanket if you are covered up. Feel your toes touching each other. This may create a tingling sensation. If you feel pain or numbness, don't resist the feeling. Simply observe it as it is.

- As you inhale, imagine your breath traveling from your nose down to your toes, and then imagine the air flowing back up and out the nose with each exhale. Maintain your focus on your toes in this way for several minutes.

- If your mind wanders and you lose concentration on the body, that's perfectly fine. Noticing that you were not aware brings instant awareness. All you have to do is bring your attention back to the particular body part and resume concentration. If you lose focus a hundred times, gently bring your attention back to the body a hundred times.

- Next, move on to the rest of the foot and offer it the same undivided attention.

- Continue this routine of concentration and breathing into each body part. A typical pattern is (1) left toes, (2) left foot, (3) left ankle, (4) left calf, (5) left shin, (6) left knee, (7) left thigh, (8) right toes, (9) right foot, (10) right ankle, (11) right calf, (12) right shin, (13) right knee, (14) right thigh, (15) hips and buttocks, (16) abdomen, (17) chest, (18) back, (19) left arm, (20) left hand, (21) left fingers, (22) right arm, (23) right hand, (24) right fingers, (25) neck, shoulders, throat, (26) top of head, and (27) face.

- Once awareness has been brought to your face, draw your attention to your nostrils and focus on the sensations of breathing.

- After a few moments direct your attention to your whole body and the sensations that may be occurring.

- When you're ready, conclude by opening your eyes slowly and expanding your awareness to the room around you.

Sitting meditation. Often referred to as "breath meditation," or simply "sitting," sitting meditation is the heart of formal meditation. It can be done in a chair or on the floor. Sitting on the floor is often preferred because of its reassuring feeling of being "grounded." It's not what you sit on, however, that counts. It's all about your sincerity to practice.

Posture is important. Your back, neck, and head should be straight and aligned vertically in a position that embodies dignity. Your shoulders and arms should be relaxed, and your hands should be in a comfortable, supported position, perhaps on your knees or in your lap.

Unlike the body scan, which moves attention through the body, the primary object of focus is always your breath.

- Sit comfortably in your chair or cushion. Experiment with your posture until your spine and head feel aligned and you feel a sense of dignity. If you're on the floor, try choosing a cushion that lifts you four to six inches off the ground. This helps align the spine more effortlessly and ease back pain.

- Begin breathing normally. Don't alter your breath in anyway. As you breathe, notice where the strongest sensations occur, and make that point your primary object of focus. It may be at the tip of your nostrils, chest, or abdomen.

- Observe the breath as it flows in and out. Give full attention to each inhalation and the slight pause that occurs at the peak of each in-breath. Next direct your full attention to each exhalation and the pause that occurs just before your next breath. Repeat this pattern, considering each breath a new beginning.

- If you notice that your mind has wandered, gently bring your attention back to the breath as you take notice of what you were thinking about. Do this each time your mind wanders. Don't be discouraged if it happens a lot. It's perfectly normal.

We recommend you use an audio recording if you are new to the practice.

Common Distractions During Meditation

Here we discuss five physical and mental diversions you may experience while practicing meditation. Addressing these diversions is important not only for meditation but also for daily life. Any of these distractions can be experienced at any time during any activity.

1. **Aversion.** Just as with life, you will encounter things you dislike during meditation and things you want to avoid, reject, or repress. The most common aversion is physical pain; others include uncomfortable emotions and even itching. Mindfulness isn't limited to optimal health and comfort. Remember that the purpose of meditation is to develop mindfulness, to focus intently on the present moment—whatever that may be.

2. The present will often be painful. If it is, temporarily make pain your object of focus. Direct your attention to how it feels rather than what your thoughts say it should feel like. Aversion to pain is often more painful than pain itself. Instead of resisting physical pain, uncomfortable emotions, or a stinging itch, try to resist your habitual desire to make discomfort go away. Discomfort is a physical and mental state, and all physical and mental states are worthy of investigation.

Get to know discomfort better. Develop a new relationship with it. Does it move around? Does it burn, or is it a dull ache? Does it pulse? Does it sting? Perhaps you feel anxious. How does anxiety affect you physically? Does it increase your heart rate and blood pressure? Where does it settle? In your chest? Your shoulders? Your jaw? Simply observe the discomfort as it peaks and then fades. Eventually it may even disappear. When it does, return your attention to your original object of focus.

3. **Desire.** It's typical to experience deep relaxation, euphoric sensations, and pleasurable thoughts while meditating. You should not seek these gratifying states, however. Many people experience a pleasing state during meditation and then try to achieve the same feeling next time around. This leads to mindless thinking about memories of past meditations and fantasies about achieving a desired state. The purpose of meditation is not to experience warm, fuzzy feelings. The purpose is to foster mindfulness of the present—even if you wish the present to be different. Desire is a mental state, and all mental states are worthy of investigation. When you notice that desire has disrupted mindful attention, simply focus on the state. Notice its strength. Eventually it will fade and disappear, at which point you can return to your original object of focus.

4. **Drowsiness.** Sleepiness is a significant issue for meditators; it's an occupational hazard. Just sitting still with closed eyes can be enough to make you nod off. This can greatly affect the concentration needed to remain mindful, and you may find yourself struggling to resist the feeling. The purpose of meditation is to promote awareness of the present moment. Sometimes the here and now is sleepy, and that's fine. Drowsiness is a physical state, and all physical states are worthy of investigation. Instead of resisting, take some time to get to know drowsiness. Often you will snap out of drowsiness by applying wakeful concentration to it. If, however, you find you are fighting to stay awake, don't

be afraid to sit or stand up. Don't meditate lying down if you're sleepy.

5. **Restlessness.** This is the most common distraction you will face during meditation. Time and again, thoughts will come to mind such as *I'm ready to get up. I have things to do. How much time is left? Should I peek at the clock? I can't remember if I paid the power bill.* Some days you will sit confidently with a tranquil mind, and some days you will sit with a restless, unsettled mind that wants to be anywhere but where you are. Restlessness, however, is merely a mental state, and all mental states are worthy of investigation. Make it your temporary object of focus. How strong is it? Where does it set up shop in your body? Look for ways to encounter agitation. Watch it rise and fall. Eventually it will fade into the background, and you can return your attention to your original object of focus.

6. **Doubt.** At some point you will be faced with thoughts such as *What am I doing sitting here? Can this really help me?* These kinds of thoughts can quickly spread to *Is there hope for me? Am I wasting time and money on counseling? Will I always be unhappy?* The mind is used to being in control, and it will do what it can to keep you from deviating from the habitual, mindless life you typically live. Feelings of doubt are just a diversion your mind uses to keep you stuck in your head and out of the present. When facing doubt, temporarily make it your object of focus. Doubt is a mental state, and all mental states are worthy of investigation. See it form, rise, and fall. Once it's gone, return your focus to your original object of focus.

Using Racing Thoughts as an Object of Focus

Calming the mind is no easy task. Some forms of meditation attempt to stop the mind from thinking. This is impossible—and not the purpose of mindfulness meditation. The purpose is always to be mindful of what is occurring in the moment, no matter what it may be. Let's say your mind is running amuck, and you can't seem to attend to your breath for longer than a couple of seconds. In this case, thinking is what is occurring in the present moment. Therefore, make thoughts your temporary object of focus, and return to the breath once the mind calms. If you can't beat them, join them.

Thoughts are like children. They're capable of nasty things when left unattended. If a child craves attention, he'll scream, whine, throw a tantrum—anything to be acknowledged. It's easy to be frustrated by such an annoyance, but it's not wise to lose control or leave him unattended. The louder you scream, the louder he screams back. Likewise, avoiding him only leads to more frustration as he strives harder to get your attention. Peace will soon return, however, if you just let him show you his toy, do his cartwheel, or tell you whatever he needs to get off his chest.

The same can be said of your thoughts. Instead of exhausting yourself trying to silence your mind or keeping your thoughts at bay, turn your attention to what your thoughts are trying to tell you. You may be surprised at how quickly they will calm. If you doubt this, close your eyes right now, and wait for your next thought to appear.

Did you notice how bashful your thoughts became all of a sudden? Chances are that it took a while for a thought to finally appear.

Both of the formal practices discussed in this chapter require you to focus on your breathing or a specific body part. You may experience extended moments of mental stillness, but this tranquility is always short-lived. Thoughts will eventually come pouring back into your mind, and your attention will be swept away. Soon you will be aware that you were lost in thought and will return your attention to your object of focus. When this happens repeatedly, it's easy to get frustrated. Don't be. This is a crucial part of practicing.

As you bring your attention back to your object of focus, take a moment to acknowledge what you were thinking about. This will quickly reveal patterns in your way of thinking. You may realize, *Wow! I had no idea I thought about _____ so much.* Or *Wow! I had no idea my thoughts were so negative and fearful.* Thoughts are not your enemy in meditation. Your goal is to mindfully attend to your object. But when mindfulness is lost, use the distraction to learn more about your way of thinking.

Developing Mindfulness Outside of Mediation

Meditation is a wonderful practice, but its benefits fade unless you commit to cultivating mindfulness day to day. To do this you must snap out of mindless thinking as often as possible and live more intentionally in the moment. This can be done anytime and anywhere by connecting with the here and now as intentionally as you do during meditation and holding the focus. Physical and environmental awareness can be strengthened outside of meditation any number of ways. Here are recommendations to get you started:

- Get dressed with your eyes closed.

- Use your opposite hand when using a TV remote, dialing a phone, or brushing your teeth.

- If you wear contacts or glasses, remove them when you are at home for the night and going about your nightly routine. Allow the decline of your sense of sight to enhance your other senses.

- Prepare and cook your own food instead of eating out or picking up meals. There is a lot of beauty in a pot or pan of cooking food—thousands of bubbles from boiling liquids; vibrant colors of vegetables; steam rising up, almost dancing; warmth radiating from the stove.

- Opt out of using your dishwasher a few nights a week. Instead, wash your dirty dishes by hand. Focus closely on the warmth of the water, the suds on your skin, and the sweet smell of the soap.

- A shower is a blast to the senses and a great way to clear your head. Next time you take a shower, give yourself over to the warmth of the water, the sound of the water spraying and gurgling down the drain, and the sweet smell of shampoo, conditioner, soap, shaving cream, and whatever else you may use.

- Eat something you enjoy. Don't work while you eat. Don't read. Turn off your phone, computer, or TV. As you eat, slow down, mute your mind, and relax your body. Give your undivided attention to the movements of your arm slowly lifting the fork to your mouth and your jaw opening and closing as you chew. Direct your attention to the taste, and savor each bite and the flavor it brings.

- Do yoga. Yoga is an excellent exercise that is also great for body awareness.

- Pick one thing you do every day, something mundane that you take for granted like opening doors, sitting down, or shaking hands. Designate such an insignificant action to trigger mindfulness. For example, every time you open a door, give yourself completely to that moment. How does it feel to wrap your hand around the doorknob and twist? When you swing the door open, do you feel a faint gust of air blow past you? When you close it, feel the vibrations in your hand as the door connects with the frame. Offer this kind of attention to whatever you choose. (By the way, you don't have to act weird while doing this. You don't have to move in slow motion or anything. If you choose to designate opening doors for mindfulness, open and close them just as you normally would. The point is to focus on your body during the action, not to draw unnecessary attention to yourself.)

- Go for a walk outside. Nature offers unlimited stimulants to direct your attention.

- When you're speaking with someone, focus more on what he or she is saying and the sound of the person's voice rather than just daydreaming mindlessly until it's your turn to talk. Think before you respond. Offer kind, mindful dialogue.

- Stop what you're doing right now and listen to the sounds happening around you. Do you hear a computer humming, kids playing in the distance, a television in the next room, or even the sound of silence?

Maybe you have a mind that prefers time traveling to the future. Or perhaps you prefer keeping an eye on what's behind you. If you're always looking down the road ahead or back to the way you have come for a solution to your current condition, a priority check may be in order. This is not to say there's anything wrong with looking ahead or back where you came from. After all, you're in counseling because you're dissatisfied with what you've already experienced, and you hope to become a stronger, healthier person. Just don't forget that what you do in the moment, the steps you are taking right now, determine your hope for the future. As you progress through counseling, try focusing more on each step you are taking and less on the goals you've set or the ones you've broken. Many clients are so fixed on what's ahead and behind that they don't realize their feet are sinking in the mire that is their current lives. Always remember that healing has less to do with beginnings and destinations; it's more about the journey.

I encourage you to practice mindfulness meditation regularly. The benefits of mindfulness meditation can be found only from doing it. It's difficult to develop a routine. In fact, this is the most difficult part for many. I advise you to pick a time and place and practice as routinely as possible. And above all, remember that all you have is the present.

Chapter 5 ⟶

Journaling:
Learning How to Process and Examine Your Heart

> O my soul, bless GOD.
>   From head to toe, I'll bless his holy name!
> O my soul, bless GOD,
>   don't forget a single blessing!
>
> — PSALM 103:1–2

Keeping a journal of what's going on in your life is a good way to help interpret and process what is important and what is not. Journaling was scary for me at first. Seeing my thoughts on paper felt too vulnerable, but the process of putting things on paper led to this book. It helped me process my emotions and thoughts nonjudgmentally. Compassion fatigue, stress, trauma, and conflict change the way we see the world. Creating a safe place to process through your journal can be a good start to getting your life back.

The Importance of Journaling

Trauma and stress have numerous side effects, one being a weakened capacity to express yourself. To grow and process stress and burnout in our chaotic world, you must address your inability to be honest with *you*. You may desire to be truthful with your thoughts and emotions, but you may not know how to express your feelings. Such ability takes work and a willingness to open up as thoughts and emotions come to the surface of your mind. The best way to develop this skill is to pay closer attention to your troublesome thoughts as they occur. Moments of clarity, emotions, and questions will certainly arise, and it's crucial to capture and record these moments. For many people the best way to accomplish this is through writing. In this chapter you'll learn how to use writing to express yourself in counseling sessions and during times of contemplation.

Journaling can help you gain insight into what you have recorded. It can help you better understand the thoughts, emotions, and relationships you hide from others and to which you are sometimes blinded. One tool that can help you understand the goal of journaling is the chapter. In 1955 Joseph Luft and Harry Ingham created this psychological tool to aid personal understanding, self-awareness, and development. At its most basic, the Johari Window helps people recognize their self-perception and the perception others have of them. Think of it as four windowpanes:

1. **Open area** – What you know about yourself and is known by others

2. **Blind spot** – What you do not know about yourself but others know

3. **Façade** – What you know about yourself but others do not know

4. **Unknown** – What is unknown about you by yourself and unknown by others

Ideally these panes become known as you process them. Journaling can be the first step. After you journal, take the insights and process them in your relationship with God and a safe community or team of people. Processing your insights can help you build trust with others by revealing information about yourself. You can also learn more about yourself by receiving feedback, love, and support from others as you discover how they perceive you. Sometimes we need a mirror to understand ourselves.

Open area: **Known to self** **Known to others**	**Blind spot:** **Unknown to self** **Known by others**
The first pane is referred to as "open." This pane represents the actions, behaviors, and information that are known to you and those around you. The information is public and made available through communication and exchanges between you and others. It includes facts, skills, and attitudes—anything that is public knowledge.	The second pane is called "blind" or "blind spot." Actions and behaviors in the blind area are known to others, but you are not aware of them. The information in the blind spot can be positive or negative and include hidden strengths or areas for improvement. It can be an excellent starting point for development.
Façade or hidden self: **Known to self** **Unknown to others**	**Unknown:** **Unknown to self** **Unknown to others**
The third pane is called "hidden" or "façade." This information is private and known to you but not to anyone else. You choose to it keep hidden. Feelings, ambitions, dreams, and opinions may be withheld from your community out of fear of negative reaction. Once you trust others, you may choose to reveal some of your hidden information.	The last window is called simply "unknown." This includes information, skills, behaviors, and so on that are unknown to you and others. It includes subconscious information such as early childhood memories or undiscovered talents of which no one is aware.

Why You Should Journal

Journaling can help you process your thoughts and emotions. It can be used in conjunction with counseling, small groups, friends, and your relationship with God. Out of the 168 hours in a week, however, it's likely you'll sit across from others for only little of that time. In such a short time it's impossible to say everything you need to say, especially if you're one of the countless people reluctant to speak openly about feelings in front of others. Through journaling you can focus more on your relationships, emotions, and thoughts, leading to an understanding of areas to which you are blinded.

Sadly, many of us can be like Israel and forget all that God has done. There are many scriptural examples of how the Israelites lost focus. Examples include Judges 8:34, Psalm 106:21, and Hosea 8:14. Journaling can help you remember, process, and focus on what God has done in your life and the lives of others. Through journaling you can contemplate what God has done and remember God's grace in your life.

Trauma and stressors are capable of shattering your life. Your goal, with the help of God and others, is to pick up the scattered pieces of your broken life. A mistake many of us make is to be too narrow in our focus; we see only the pain or the problem. We focus too strongly on the tiny shards of shattered happiness, lacking the ability to step outside of pain and behold the big picture. Journaling is a way to collect the pieces and bind them back together. For many people, conceptualizing thoughts and emotions purely in the mind is difficult. Sometimes seeing your questions, thoughts, and epiphanies on paper helps you see where you are weakest and strongest.

How Journaling Affects Health

We have already discussed the negative, long-lasting effects of stress on your body, especially the immune system. Studies have shown that writing about trauma and stress can improve the body's resilience. People who write about their deepest, most traumatic thoughts and feelings experience heightened immune function compared with those who write merely about superficial topics (Pennebaker 1997).

Other studies link writing to decreased blood pressure by helping to moderate the expression of destructive emotions like intense anger or fright. Journaling can reduce anger levels, thus lowering blood pressure in people prone to anger. In addition, regular journaling has a sustainable benefit, as it can lighten your load, help you keep a positive outlook, cultivate your social relationships, and steer you clear of self-induced conflicts (Lepore and Smyth 2002).

Many people find it difficult to express themselves with words, so they hold them in. Such tension can lead to long-term health risks. Sometimes your feelings may be too strong to spontaneously articulate to another person, such as a therapist. Or the weight of your thoughts may be too heavy to get off your chest. Think of the act of writing as taking the weight of the world and putting it on paper.

Personally I've never liked journaling. I've always struggled putting my words to paper. In fact, even writing *this* brings some discomfort! But I've learned to accept writing as a source of clarity, direction, and peace to process jumbled thoughts and emotions. Often it's hard to push through initial feelings, but I've found if I relax and keep trying, the benefits are substantial.

Just because I don't like journaling doesn't mean I don't believe in its power. In fact, I recommend it to clients all the time. Let's say, for example, I am working with you on relaxation during a session. I may ask you to journal each day about your experience with the act and process of relaxing. Simply by writing about your experience, you are more likely to return the next week with a deeper understanding.

I didn't start journaling until several years ago. In fact, keeping a diary led to my interest in writing. I've found that writing down thoughts is the best way for me to flesh out the ideas in my head. Other than mindfulness, writing is perhaps the most therapeutic exercise I've found to date.

Tips on How to Journal

Journals are a dime a dozen these days. They were once limited to bound paper. The nicer ones included a lock and key to keep others out. Today it's more common for someone to use an online journal or blog site. The lock and key have been replaced by a username and password. Paper has been replaced by storage space somewhere on a distant server. The medium you choose by which to write your feelings, however, is not important. It is strictly a personal preference.

The goal is to capture any thought, any emotion, at any time. I recommend that you carry a small notepad or a text app on your phone or PDA to jot down ideas as they come to you throughout the day. Later, when you sit down with your journal, use your notes to spark your memory. Without this, many realizations may be lost. Taking notes encourages spontaneity—an important healing quality lacked by many people because of anxiety or depression. Without a commitment to logging spontaneous moments of clarity, you will likely repress or forget what you've learned, stifling forward momentum.

A journal doesn't have to be written well. The point is simply to get your thoughts out in the open. Think of every entry as a rough draft. Keep writing and don't stop until you're done. The point isn't to use proper grammar and punctuation. Correct spelling pales in comparison with simply emptying yourself. In fact, trying to write well and revisiting your writing with the purpose of editing or revising can be detrimental to the integrity of what you were feeling when you originally wrote it. You may water down your passion or over-embellish. Keep it simple and true.

Journaling is a personal act. There is no right or wrong way to record your thoughts. You don't have to be consistent with a technique to expect consistent results. The simple act of writing will help slow your mind, change your perspective, and teach you new things about yourself. Journaling's ability to put thoughts and feelings into words is a powerful therapy tool. Recording memories, fears, concerns, and problems helps relieve stress and promote health and leads to personal growth.

There's a good chance you may sit down with your new journal and find yourself staring cluelessly at blank pages with no idea of how to write the first sentence, much less your whole story. Or perhaps you lack the time and privacy to properly empty yourself on paper. If this happens, don't be discouraged. There are ways to develop active, productive writing.

Ways to Get the Most from Writing

First, let me state there is no one right way to journal. There is no evidence that journaling at the beginning of your day is any more effective than journaling at the end of your day. It is not necessary to begin with your most painful or terrifying experiences. Rather, begin with your current dilemma or emotion. Write about the anxiety you felt today or something that made you uncomfortable. If your thoughts continually return to a particular event or experience—maybe a hurtful statement made by a loved one earlier in the day—make this your first topic to write about. Perhaps you want to confront someone or confess a secret, but you just can't bring yourself to say it aloud, much less to the intended person. Use your journal to practice expressing heavy words. Your confession on paper can be fine-tuned to develop a mental script.

Once your first few sentences are written, your creativity will likely emerge. As your thoughts begin to flow, be mindful to relive the experience you're writing about. What happened? How did you feel in that instance? How do you feel about it now? Why do you feel that way?

You may occasionally need time off from writing; this is perfectly fine. Writing about painful instances every day can be overwhelming and draining and should never be a substitute for action or a way to avoid responsibility. You shouldn't assume that only negative experiences are to be fleshed out. Be sure to devote time to writing about positive experiences, both past and present. Write out your most meaningful life experiences and opinions. Also, don't feel pressured to write only about things that evoke emotion. Try writing out your goals and priorities, and develop potential methods to dedicate more time to them or to see them fulfilled (Lepore and Smyth 2002).

Where you choose to write may or may not be influential. You may be the type of person who can write in a busy room with screaming kids, or this may be impossible. You won't know until you try. We recommend, however, that you to find a secluded spot where you won't be bothered by unwanted sounds, sights, or smells.

Different Journaling Styles

Let's discuss a few journaling styles.

Gratitude journal. This is a newer form of journaling that comes from positive psychology. The basic practice is straightforward. Just start simple by recording five things you experienced over the past week for which you feel grateful. The entries can be brief, sometimes just a single sentence. Studies about gratitude journals have shown a range of significant benefits, including better sleep, fewer symptoms of illness, and more happiness among adults and children (Emmons and McCullough 2003).

Robert Emmons, a professor at the University of California, Davis, gives some research-based suggestions for getting the best benefits from your gratitude journal. The focus of the gratitude journal is on good, positive, happy things in your life that you may overlook or take for granted. That is why the suggestion is to write once a week. Over time we become numb to the goodness in our lives. Create an opportunity once a week to dwell on the things for which you are grateful. Emmons suggests that when starting a gratitude journal, you should see each item you list as a gift to savor and relish. Take time to look at it, enjoy it, and feel the depth of the gratitude. Don't hurry through the exercise of writing a gratitude journal. It is not a to-do list but a way of experiencing and focusing on gratitude.

Emmons even points out that "research shows that translating thoughts into concrete language—whether oral or written—has advantages over just thinking the thoughts; it makes us more aware of them, deepening their emotional impact. Writing helps to organize thoughts, facilitate integration, and helps you accept your own experiences and put them in context," he says. "In essence, it allows you to see the meaning of events going on around you and create meaning in your own life" (Emmons and McCullough 2003).

Free-writing journal. The free-writing technique is simple. Just write continually. Don't stop to think about what you're expressing. Jot down whatever comes to mind without judging your thoughts or how well you're writing. With this style it's common to set a time limit, usually five to fifteen minutes. It may be a good idea to set a kitchen timer and write as fast and hard as you can until you hear the bell. Ignore any regard for spelling, grammar, and so on, and make no corrections. If you reach a point at which you can think of nothing to write, simply write sentences about how you are drawing a blank until another line of thought comes to mind—and it will.

There are two approaches. First, don't dwell on a particular topic. Let your thoughts roam where they may. Second, try revolving all your thoughts around a particular topic. Allowing your thoughts to explore the chosen topic may develop different opinions and new perspectives.

Free writing is a fantastic tool to help clear your mind and release anxious energy. You can then use the resulting tranquility to connect to your emotions and needs. Free writing helps clear the clutter in your mind as the stream of thoughts and emotions begins to flow out of you.

Diary. A diary is the traditional style typically associated with a journal. It is an ongoing, time-stamped document. A diary is different from a journal in that it should be written daily, whereas journaling can be less frequent. A diary's purpose is to record the events of your life, and its circulation is usually limited to only you or a limited few you entrust with such private information. A diary is beneficial to therapy by offering a daily perspective on pain and troubling thoughts.

Art journal. A picture is worth a thousand words, right? If you find your words aren't doing justice to your intense emotions, try drawing or painting what you feel. Just as in free-writing exercises, draw whatever comes to mind no matter how bizarre or inartistic. Pictures, doodles, and even stick figures will eventually open up the flow of words and thoughts. As you draw, a strong word may come to the surface of your mind. When this happens, scribble it down before you forget it, and continue your art. Soon you may find more words appearing and forming into sentences and ideas. Before you know it, you're expressing yourself in ways you never dreamed possible.

You may be good with words but bad at expressing yourself. If so, don't limit art journaling to only drawing or painting. Try picking a topic that inspires you and write a free-form poem. Don't let the word *poem* discourage you. It doesn't have to rhyme or have a certain style. The idea is simply to express your feelings artistically. Another approach is to write a fictional short story about a character who shares your struggle. Helping this character deal with his or her problems may prove beneficial to your own circumstances.

Letter journal. Letter journaling is a powerful technique that has contributed to the healing of many. The method is simple: you write letters to family, friends, enemies—both living and dead—or imaginary characters who represent the strong emotions you feel. A letter journal creates the opportunity to tell someone your feelings and thoughts without the conflict of a face-to-face encounter. The usual intent of the letters is not to give them to the people to whom they are addressed; they are for you to resolve conflict or loss within yourself.

Reflecting on Your Journal

Reflecting may be easy for some but scary for others. If you cringe at the idea of opening your journal, much less reading your work aloud, it would be a good practice to bring your journal to your sessions for your counselor to read if you are comfortable doing so. If you write in an online diary, you may allow your counselor to pull it up on his or her computer. This is a priceless tool for any mental health professional—to view the inner workings of your mind expressed in true honesty.

Fear of expressing yourself may simply come from a lack of knowing how. To gain experience, allow your counselor to view your work and walk you through ways to reflect more comfortably. Just hearing someone read back what you wrote may be liberating, leading to more confidence for expressing yourself in the real world.

When to Stop Journaling

As you grow healthier, it's normal if your journaling habits begin to slow, although you may see the benefit of journaling every day for the rest of your life. For most people, however, journal entries become few and far between as time passes. As you empty yourself and the pieces of your life are reassembled, there may be less to express on paper. For many people, this is a sign that growth is occurring.

You may wonder what to do with the countless pages when you conclude your final entry. Some people throw them onto a bookshelf and revisit them later as a trophy of success. Others experience a powerful sense of closure by tearing up or burning the documents once they experience a breakthrough. Whether stored away in your attic, on a shelf, or smoldering in ashes, your journal serves one final purpose: a tangible statement of how far you've come and the freedom you have worked so hard to accomplish.

Chapter 6 →

Self-Talk:
Learning to Change Your Thoughts

> We demolish arguments and every pretension that sets itself up against the knowledge of God, and we take captive every thought to make it obedient to Christ.
>
> — 2 Corinthians 10:5 NIV

> We have two options: we can live in the beautiful reality of who we really are, or we can live in a debilitating delusion.
>
> — Andrew Farley

We are daily influenced by thousands of images and voices in the world around us that affect our mood, thoughts, and behavior. Many times we fail to recognize how we are talking to ourselves and lose the importance of controlling our thoughts and self-talk. We need to recognize that we are constantly talking to ourselves, commenting internally on everything we encounter. Sadly, we believe the negative self-talk because of our interpretation of the world around us, an interpretation based on a negative past or present. We have power over that voice and how it affects us, though at times it does not feel that way. But we can change the voice into something that gives instead of takes.

Paul David Tripp makes an important point in his daily devotional *New Morning Mercies* when he writes, "No one is more influential in your life than you are, because no one talks to you more than you do. We never stop talking to ourselves.... The things you say to you about you, God, and life are profoundly important because they form and shape the way you then respond to the things that God has put on your plate" (Tripp 2014).

Self-Talk

Self-talk is the evolving conversation we have with ourselves in our mind. This conversation includes thoughts about ourselves, such as *I'm worthless* or *I'm not good at this*. It also includes thoughts about our environment and lives, such as *I'll be stuck in this job forever* or *This will completely ruin my day*. We all have these kinds of continuous conversations with ourselves. We may not always be aware of it, but these conversations have a considerable impact on our mood, behavior, and relationships.

You've likely noticed a recurring idea throughout the book that thoughts deceive, oppress, and belittle. More often than not, if you took your thoughts out of your head and gave them a voice, they would sound exactly like the abusive people of your past. You would certainly retaliate against anyone who talked to you so hatefully. So why cower when it's you who is the bully?

I think we have three voices in our head. The question is what voice we hear the loudest. The three voices and what they sound like are

- **God**—Loving, encouraging, guiding, and not condemning. He always offers solutions.

- **Ourselves**—Many times we bully ourselves like the negative condemning people of our past and sometimes our present.

- **Enemy**—Condemning, confusing, and demeaning. We always feel powerless and stuck. He offers no solutions; we are just condemned.

To understand the effect on your daily life of each of these voices would require multiple books and conversations. The focus of this small chapter on self-talk is your voice and how it affects self-care. We sound like an inner bully when we experience stress and conflict. When we are living in a hectic, stressful environment, the inner negative voice becomes louder.

Throughout this chapter I use the term *inner bully* to describe our negative self-talk. I use this term because, as with all bullies, you have to confront, challenge, and redirect them. The inner bully of our self-talk comes from our past, especially authority figures. My hope is that this chapter helps you begin to hear self-talk sounds like God's affirmation from Scripture.

To get rid of a thought, you have to replace it with another thought. This sounds simplistic, but it is vital and sometimes complex. You have the power to defeat the negative inner self-talk.

This chapter brings a powerful memory to mind. Before I considered pursuing counseling as my profession, I was once sitting in a counseling session where my counselor taught me to question my thoughts—my irrational beliefs—and believe a truer reality. This freedom came as I learned to treat myself with love and compassion. Basically I stopped beating myself up. Honestly, if I had not experienced that session, I would not be writing this today. The freedom I experienced was powerful enough to begin my journey toward helping people for a living. As a professional counselor, I come to work every day hoping to show people they don't have to talk negatively to themselves.

The revelation is that you get to talk to yourself any way you choose. You can be your greatest source of pain or your greatest source of encouragement. The choice is yours. Positive self-talk may be the hardest good habit to develop. It always feels much better to affirm yourself and believe you are worthy instead of constantly keeping a negative self-image.

What We Mean by the Inner Bully

You have little control over what comes to your mind. Thoughts constantly appear, and they typically do and say whatever they please. They can be pleasant and light one minute and then oppress, assault, and deceive you the next, often for no apparent reason. Your brain has intrusive thoughts that can sound like a bully, and your mind will go out of its way to intentionally cause you pain. Given that you're in counseling or considering counseling, it is safe to assume that you have come face-to-face with your inner bully. This is the part of your mind that lies to you, cheats you out of happiness, and keeps you on edge because you never know when or where he will strike.

You can run but you can't hide from your inner bully. Even if you focus your attention on a certain thing or intentionally recall a particular memory, your brain will soon trail off and carry you somewhere else. (If you have practiced the mindfulness meditation techniques mentioned in chapter 4, you have seen the truth of this firsthand.) The mind incessantly and involuntarily explores, relives past events, fantasizes, and calculates. Though it encourages and praises at times, it is capable of producing insults. Often these reveries lead you down a dark alley where the bully appears from the shadows.

But the bully does not appear in a vacuum. He was conceived and is sustained by the harmful words of others. He is strengthened by your own insecurities. Notice how the bully amplifies and reverberates the words of others. It's bad enough when a loved one insults you; it can be unbearable when you also have to deal with the echo of that person's voice in your head. The sting of the initial offense lives on long after the spoken word. Your mind keeps the pain alive, replaying the hurtful moment hundreds of times—even if the person offended you only once. Imagine how stressful it would be if your insulter were to shout the same hateful phrase at you hundreds of times a day. Little do you realize, this is exactly what your bully does. You're just used to it. It's habitual, and it's been happening for a very long time. You've heard the bully all your life. It's time to question whether his words are true.

From birth, other people have contributed to your self-image. People use words to describe your looks, work ethic, intelligence, athleticism, artistic ability, and so on. Other people's words impact how you talk about yourself and cause you to believe things that are untrue.

For example, let's say your mother raised you from birth to believe in a particular image of the world—that the earth is flat—and you believe it wholeheartedly. Does that make it true? Absolutely not. A brief period of inquiry and research would reveal that the earth is, in fact, round. For thousands of years this very idea caused people to believe a ship would sail off the edge of the earth if it ventured too far out at sea. The thought of a flat earth limited the potential of sailors who believed it, preventing them from discovering a "new world."

Similarly, if your mother told you from birth that you're stupid, does that make it true? Again, absolutely not. The truth is that you are an intelligent person, but your bully keeps spinning deceit in your head as it repeats your mother's words, "You're stupid! You're stupid!" Such badgering makes it nearly impossible to investigate undiscovered truth about yourself, thus greatly limiting your potential.

How have people's words and other outside influences fashioned your self-image? How do they limit you? Are their words true to who you are? How do you talk to yourself as a result?

How the Inner Bully Reacts to the Words of Others

When someone speaks to you in a way that causes insult or discouragement, you typically respond in one of four ways:

1. accommodating the bully

2. dismissing, denying, or avoiding the bully

3. becoming the bully

4. facing the bully

Accommodating the bully. When you accommodate the bully, you accept the threatening information without question. Your mind then rearranges your current identities to make room for this new data. Such unbridled acceptance causes previously held positive identities to be thrown out to make room for new hurtful ideas. This shift in information also causes a shift in thought. Your mind no longer echoes praise. It now prompts unsettlement and embarrassment, and these feelings begin deteriorating your self-identity. We recommend you not take this response; it encourages the bully to continue tormenting you because you show no effort to defend yourself.

Dismissing, denying, or avoiding the bully. Dismissing, denying, or avoiding the bully is certainly better than simply embracing insult and allowing him to run rampant. Rejection of the threatening information, however, can lessen your chances of learning anything about yourself. This approach makes it difficult for you to investigate the truth behind hurtful words as you push them away from your inquiring mind. With this response, the bully in your brain is likely to be outraged by your avoidance. He will grow louder and more severe in an attempt to be heard, and he will continue until either satisfied or defeated by your response.

Becoming the bully. Becoming the bully is a case of "If you can't beat them, join them." For example, you're offended because your boss tells you that you were not chosen for a promotion. Your thoughts instantly bombard you with memories of being denied. Only in this case, you strike back instead of accommodating or ignoring thoughts about what your boss said. You become agitated and angry as you argue with yourself and the person in your head. You repeat the phrase and words in a way that you become the bully. Your thoughts are no longer hurtful; they are angry. Now they encourage you, but not in a healthy way. Rather, they entice you either to engage in fantasies about how you could return pain on your insulter or to embrace the role of the bully and ruthlessly attach to reasons why you aren't good enough or don't deserve the job. In this case you become your own worst enemy. With this response the bully remains at large and is guaranteed to incite a similar scenario the next time you face threatening information.

Facing the bully. The bully exists. There's no denying that. It's time to silence him. But remember: he's sneaky. He hides in the shadows, repeatedly shouting insults and waiting to strike. You have to find him to confront him, and most people look for him in all the wrong places.

The bully does not dwell in the event that insulted you or in the emotions you feel as a result. For example, when your boss denies you the promotion, you might think, *I'm angry because my boss did not give me the job.* You think there are only two components to the problem: (1) rejection that leads to (2) anger. There is, however, a missing link, a third element. The bully is not in the rejection or the anger; he is in between. He is in the irrational beliefs you tell yourself, such as *I didn't get the job because my boss is a jerk, I'm a failure,* or *My boss doesn't like me, and neither does anyone else.* The anger doesn't spring from the rejection; it results from your beliefs about being rejected. The bully dwells in these irrational beliefs. To shut him up you must investigate the truth behind these beliefs.

Here are some common terms your counselor may use when referring to irrational beliefs.

1. **All-or-nothing thinking:** *Since I didn't get the promotion, I am not good at anything.*

2. **Jumping to conclusions:** *Since I didn't get the promotion, my boss thinks I'm an idiot.*

3. **Fortune-telling:** *Since I didn't get the promotion, I will never succeed at anything.*

4. **Focusing on the negative:** *Since I didn't get the promotion, I can see nothing good happening in my life.*

5. **Disqualifying the positive:** *Because I didn't get the promotion, I know my boss is only being kind when he compliments my work. He doesn't mean it.*

6. **"Allness" and "neverness":** *Since I should have received the promotion but didn't, I will always feel angry and never be happy.*

7. **Minimization:** *Any success I've had was just good luck and not important. I never deserved any of it. But my mistakes, which never should have happened and led to not getting the promotion, are awful and unforgivable.*

8. **Emotional reasoning:** *I didn't get the promotion, so I am a failure. The fact that I feel so bad is proof that I'm no good at all.*

9. **Labeling and overgeneralizing:** *Because I should have gotten the promotion but didn't, I am a loser.*

10. **Perfectionism:** *I realize I did fairly well to be considered for the promotion, but I should have been perfect. I am therefore incompetent* (DiGiuseppe and Doyle 2001).

Perhaps you notice a familiar irrational belief from the list above. If so, your counselor would be grateful to hear about it in your next session. A lively, therapeutic conversation would surely follow.

Facing the bully is the basis for positive self-talk. It is the act of investigating the untruths of irrational beliefs and learning to state the opposite. Simply put, expressing positive aspects about yourself in a loving, gentle, and compassionate manner counteracts the bully. It strips him of power to harm.

I didn't get the promotion because someone else was more qualified. My boss likes me, and I like him. I'm a reliable, proficient employee, and my coworkers are good people. I am still capable of attaining my goals, and they will come in time. Until then, I will make the most of my days and be the best person I can be.

There is no room for your bully in this statement. Such simple words are powerful to build self-worth and bring balance to your troubled mind. Think of positive self-affirmation as killing your inner bully with kindness by using support, kindness, and tenderness.

The Self-Talking Cure

Limited research has been conducted on the therapeutic value of positive self-talk. A recent study, however, examined whether using positive self-affirmation could reduce stress. In the study, two groups of volunteers were given a task to complete. Once the task was done, everyone was informed that he or she performed poorly on the task. One group filled out a self-affirmation worksheet after receiving the bad news, and the other group did not. The participants who filled out the worksheet were said to contemplate less on failure, suggesting that positive self-talk can decrease stressful thinking (Dutcher 2012).

If positive self-affirmations are shown to reduce anxiety, then it is reasonable that repeated affirmations could be useful tools for facing daily stressors. Stress impacts more than just the mind. It can also devastate the body, especially the immune system. (This topic is discussed in chapter 5.) In this regard, a daily self-affirmation intervention could lead to a healthier lifestyle.

Unfortunately, we rarely enjoy silence. Even when we are alone, away from the hustle and bustle of work and relationships, we are always talking to ourselves whether we want to hear it or not. Given this, it's crucial to learn to speak nicely to yourself. For many people positive inner dialogue is exercised through prayer. This inward expression can come from hopes, dreams, sacred writings, or an affirmation example you received along the way.

If it's impossible to stop the constant conversation with yourself, the goal should instead be to gain control of the conversation, not allowing the bully to dominate the dialogue. Become more aware of how you talk, and be more gentle and affirming with the person you talk to the most—you. The good news is you have the power to change. Bettering the way you self-talk is a choice you can make, so choose a way that encourages and affirms your values and strengths. Treat yourself better than the negative people from your past did. You don't have to be your own accuser. Instead, be you.

This may prove a better alternative than journaling if you don't like to write but don't mind talking to yourself. Just as in journaling, experiment with ways to change how you affirm yourself. You may have lacked personal awareness for so long that you now find it hard to talk to yourself. It may be like talking to a stranger. If so, don't worry. You have the rest of your life to get to know you. Start by speaking to yourself as you would someone you value. Treat yourself with care and compassion above all else.

What You Should Say to Yourself

The key to practicing self-talk is less about words and more about an attitude of positive hope—not negative unrest. A large vocabulary is not required. Just stay positive and encouraging. Be intentional with your affirmations. Use strong, direct, and supportive statements.

This chapter concludes with a list of sample phrases to recite. However, don't feel as though you are limited to only these. Use the examples as a starting point to develop your own voice.

An Example of a Twice-Daily Affirmation

- **Beginning of the day:** *Yesterday has come and gone. Today is a new day. It's my day. I'm strong and can trust myself to make good choices. I can do this, one moment at a time, one step at a time.*

- **End of the day:** *I did well today and I deserve to rest. The struggles of the day in no way define me, although today's events, both good and bad, taught me more about myself. When tomorrow arrives I'll take this knowledge and put it to use. I have hope because I'm strong, and tomorrow I'll have another chance to change and grow. But for right now I'm satisfied. I'm proud.*

Examples of Self-Esteem Affirmations

- I am lovable.
- I am worthy of friendship and love.

- I accept myself.

- I have a firm sense of self-identity.

- I see myself genuinely and objectively.

- I find deep tranquility within myself just as I am.

- I speak positively about myself to myself.

- I am a compassionate, caring, and honest person.

- I forgive myself for everything I've done to others or myself.

Examples of Positive Thinking Affirmations Regarding Fear

- I am not someone who thinks fearfully.

- Failure doesn't frighten me.

- I will do the things I want to do without anxiety.

- I will easily discard negative thoughts and attitudes about myself.

- I am not a fearful person.

- I expect to succeed because I am a successful, ambitious person.

- I work hard to succeed, and I will succeed because I've earned it.

These positive affirmations are wonderful, and you should use them often to redirect your thoughts. Even with that said, sometimes it is hard to make this work and have impact. I found that I can try to rationalize or minimize these affirmations away. I need to experience them in relationship with God and others. Learn to be intentional about who you spend time with. Look for people who help you see yourself in a different way, people who affirm you through their words and behaviors.

The relationship that can change how you see and talk with yourself is your relationship with Christ. I wanted to give you another list of affirmations that are harder to minimize and rationalize away. Read the list several times and note three to five verses to which you have an emotional reaction. Write down those verses and meditate on them. Read them daily and add them to your list of affirmations. I am convinced they will change the way you talk to yourself.

> *My Child,*
>
> You may not know me, but I know everything about you. (See Psalm 139:1)
>
> I know when you sit down and when you rise up. (See Psalm 139:2)
>
> I am familiar with all your ways. (See Psalm 139:3)
>
> Even the very hairs on your head are numbered. (See Matthew 10:29–31
>
> For you were made in my image. (See Genesis 1:27)
>
> In me you live and move and have your being. (See Acts 17:28)
>
> For you are my offspring. (See Acts 17:28)
>
> I knew you even before you were conceived. (See Jeremiah 1:4–5)

I chose you when I planned creation.
(See Ephesians 1:11–12)

You were not a mistake, for all your days are
written in my book. (See Psalm 139:15–16)

I determined the exact time of your birth and
where you would live. (See Acts 17:26)

You are fearfully and wonderfully made.
(See Psalm 139:14)

And brought you forth on the day you were born.
(See Psalm 71:6)

And it is my desire to lavish my love on you, simply
because you are my child and I am your father.
(See 1 John 3:1)

I offer you more than your earthly father ever
could. (See Matthew 6:31–33)

For I am the perfect father. (See Matthew 5:48)

Every good gift that you receive comes from my
hand. (See James 1:17)

For I am your provider and I meet all your needs.
(See Matthew 6:31–33)

My plan for your future has always been filled with
hope. (See Jeremiah 29:11)

Because I love you with an everlasting love.
(See Jeremiah 31:3)

My thoughts toward you are countless as the sand
on the seashore. (See Psalm 139:17–18)

And I rejoice over you with singing.
(See Zephaniah 3:17)

I will never stop doing good to you.
(See Jeremiah 32:40)

For you are my treasured possession.
(See Exodus 19:5)

I desire to establish you with all my heart and all my soul. (See Jeremiah 32:41)

And I want to show you great and marvelous things. (See Jeremiah 33:3)

If you seek me with all your heart, you will find me.
(See Deuteronomy 4:29)

Delight in me and I will give you the desires of your heart. (See Psalm 37:4)

For it is I who gave you those desires.
(See Philippians 2:13)

I am able to do more for you than you could possibly imagine. (See Ephesians 3:20)

For I am your greatest encourager.
(See 2 Thessalonians 2:16–17)

I am also the Father who comforts you in all your troubles. (See 2 Corinthians 1:3–4)

When you are brokenhearted, I am close to you.
(See Psalm 34:18)

As a shepherd carries a lamb, I have carried you close to my heart. (See Isaiah 40:11)

One day I will wipe away every tear from your eyes. (See Revelation 21:3–4)

And I'll take away all the pain you have suffered on this earth. (See Revelation 21:3–4)

I am your Father, and I love you even as I love my son, Jesus. (See John 17:26)

For in Jesus, my love for you is revealed. (See John 17:26)

He is the exact representation of my being. (See Hebrews 1:3)

He came to demonstrate that I am for you, not against you. (See Romans 8:31)

And to tell you that I am not counting your sins. (See 2 Corinthians 5:18–19)

Jesus died so that you and I could be reconciled. (See 2 Corinthians 5:18–19)

His death was the ultimate expression of my love for you. (See 1 John 4:10)

I gave up everything I loved that I might gain your love. (See Romans 8:31–32)

If you receive the gift of my son Jesus, you receive me. (See 1 John 2:23)

And nothing will ever separate you from my love again. (See Romans 8:38–39)

Come home and I'll throw the biggest party heaven has ever seen. (See Luke 15:7)

I have always been Father, and will always be Father. (See Ephesians 3:14–15)

My question is, will you be my child? (See John 1:12–13)

I am waiting for you. (See Luke 15:11–32)

Love,

Your Dad, Almighty God

Chapter 7

Come to the Table:
Connecting with God and Others

> "Come to Me, all who are weary and burdened, and I will give you rest. Take My yoke upon you and learn from Me, for I am gentle and humble in heart, and YOU WILL FIND REST FOR YOUR SOULS. For My yoke is comfortable, and My burden is light."
>
> — MATTHEW 11:28–30 NASB

> Thou hast made us for thyself, O Lord, and our heart is restless until it finds its rest in thee.
>
> — ST. AUGUSTINE

Spiritual self-care means learning to rest and trust that "You are the child of a kind, strong, and engaged Father, a Father wise enough to guide you in the Way, generous enough to provide for your journey, offering to walk with you every step. This is perhaps the hardest thing for us to believe—really believe, down deep in our hearts, so that it changes us forever, changes the way we approach each day" (John Eldredge).

The basic truth of self-care is that you need to be a good steward of your body, soul, and spirit. The hectic life we live creates isolation and distance, making it hard to live out the basic truth of self-care. Connection to God and others helps you gain perspective, feel healthy emotions again, and establish hope.

We are relational beings because we are created by a relational God. We were created in God's image, and we long for relational connection because God exists in a relationship of love. God designed us to live in relationships in which we give and receive care support and encouragement. We need one another to help carry one another's burdens in relationship. This giving and receiving is what God designed for us to experience. It gives us safety and love as we live out the great commandment to love God and our neighbor. It is vital to know that you are not alone. He has provided what you need to enjoy a life in community with Him and others.

We have an essential need for belonging. When we are faced with stress, trauma, and difficulty, we are most likely to thrive when we feel connected to significant others. Although marriage is likely the primary source of support for many of us, it is vital to maintain connections with friends and family too. Use phone calls, texts, and teleconferencing platforms like Zoom with family and friends to help navigate difficult times.

Stress, trauma, depression, and anxiety push us toward isolation and not toward relationships. Many times people withdraw and distance themselves, making it difficult for friends and family to provide support. Stress is contagious; if you don't deal with it, others will catch it. By trying to handle things on your own, you create stress and conflict for those you love. Self-care that fosters and creates space for our relational needs is vital.

Stress and trauma can impact relationships in many ways. Impacts I have observed in my own practice include

- avoidance and deterioration of emotional and physical intimacy

- withdrawal and isolation from meaningful interaction with others

- feelings of powerlessness, hopelessness, and sadness

- feelings of frustration and anger

- an increase in anxiety and depression

- more conflict, arguments, and difficulty resolving problems

It is well established that having caring and encouraging relationships reduces health risks as much or more than well-known health-promoting factors such as quitting smoking, losing weight, and engaging in regular exercise (Rippe 2018). Research confirms that people in loving, committed relationships have fewer visits to the doctor, shorter hospital stays, less chronic pain, and more positive emotions (Ong, Zautra, and Reid 2101). Positive, loving friendships also make us more resilient when hard times come. We must work hard to create or maintain good relationships, especially marriage, to make an investment in our long-term emotional and physical health.

The most important way to create life-giving self-care is relationships. Stress and trauma reduce our capacity to cope with life, but healthy connections and relationships give life and energy. We were not created to live in isolation. We need community for support, encouragement, correction, and guidance. All of us want to feel loved, wanted, and enjoyed.

Stress and trauma can distort the world in a way that feels dangerous to people and community. We are unwilling to believe that someone would want us or enjoy us.

Relationships are another way to understand yourself, as we discussed in the section on the Johari Window in chapter 5. Relationships reflect back to us who we are. They give us perspective and understanding. Their love and commitment create a safety that feels like a mirror so you can truly see yourself. Your self-care needs to include relationships that give more than they take. Here are some ways to create and maintain healthy relationships that will strengthen your perspective and understanding of yourself.

- **Maintain a self-care routine.** This may seem like an odd place to start, but happiness and health are your responsibility, not someone else's. Try to stick to regular sleep hours, waking up on time, making your bed, getting dressed each day, and eating nutritious foods. Making a priority to schedule breaks, such as a midday exercise or meditation session, can break up the day and help relationships stay grounded.

- **Spend time outside.** Look for beauty outside; it will energize and balance you heart (see Psalm 8:3–4). Go for a run or a bike ride, work in the garden, or even just take a walk together as a couple.

- **Plan for something fun.** Couples need to look for opportunities to laugh, play, encourage, affirm each other, and touch nonsexually. You can take a drive together or plan a special meal.

- **Create a gratitude journal.** Every day write three things you are grateful for about your partner or your life. This practice can be life giving and change your perspective about life (see Philippians 4:8). Learn to go overboard with compliments and gratitude to your partner and family.

- **Understand how your partner handles stress and refuels.** Become aware of what you both need to process and deal with stress and learn how to give each other space and respect as you honor those needs without questioning their validity.

Some people cannot believe that a loving community and a loving God are inviting them to the table. The table for me as a child was a place of love, acceptance, and community. The table is where we meet with people and share life. It's also a place where we meet God and connect with Him.

Tables are one of the most important places of our connection with God and others. Our hearts are most fully alive when sharing a meal around a table with those we love. It shouldn't be surprising to find that throughout the Bible, God has a way of showing up at tables. In fact, at the center of the spiritual lives of God's people in both the Old and New Testaments we find tables: the table of Passover and the table of Communion. New Testament scholar N. T. Wright captured something of this belief when he wrote, "When Jesus himself wanted to explain to his disciples what his forthcoming death was all about, he didn't give them a theory—he gave them a meal."

The key to self-care is relationship. All the tools we have laid out become exponentially stronger if you are willing to come to the table and live your life in a day-to-day relationship with God and others. Each of us comes to the table with our personality, gender, life experiences, and wounds. You are accepted, wanted, and enjoyed even with this baggage. Many times we struggle with self-care because of shame—the feeling that we don't belong. God wants you to bring all of who you are to the table and be refreshed and renewed with Him.

In his book *Sacred Pathways* author Gary Thomas shares nine spiritual temperaments, or sacred pathways, that people have. These are the pathways we use to connect with God, the tables at which we commune with God and live our relationship with Him.

1. Naturalists: Love and connect with God through nature

Naturalists feel closest to God when they're surrounded by God's creation. Being outside in the mountains, the forests, or the water awakens something in them that nothing else does. Being outdoors helps the naturalist understand scriptural truths, see and experience God more clearly, and learn to rest.

2. Sensates: Love and connect with God through the senses

Sensates feel closest to God when they are awed by the presence of beauty and when they can see, smell, hear, or almost even taste His majesty. Naturalists are drawn to God's splendor and beauty *outdoors* while sensates are drawn to *expressions* of awe and beauty through the senses. The smell or taste of coffee in the morning will draw a sensate toward an awareness of God. Beautiful artwork and music remind him or her of the greatness of God's love.

3. Traditionalists: Love and connect with God through ritual and symbols

Traditionalists are drawn to God through ritual and structure in their worship. They experience God through corporate worship that includes rituals, symbols, and the sacraments. Sacrifice is essential to their experience of a life of faith. Traditionalists are drawn to a personal rule (or habit) of life and prayer. They enjoy following and celebrating the liturgical calendar, including symbols as reminders of faith. They engage in regular, specific personal sacrifice like the spiritual disciplines. Traditionalists are drawn to these practices as life-altering experiences.

4. Ascetics: Love and connect with God in solitude and simplicity

Ascetics are attracted to solitude, simplicity, austerity, and deep commitment and sacrifice. They find that discipline and extreme plainness and simplicity, severity, and solitude awaken their souls to the presence of God. They are drawn to this as an expression of love toward God, not as a way to win His approval. They experience God's presence and love when they're alone in simplicity with nothing to distract them. The ascetics' self-denial doesn't come from a desire to be a martyr or to punish themselves, but it is a way to love and experience God more.

5. Activists: Love and connect with God through confrontation

The activists experience God's love and presence when they are standing and fighting injustice. Activists draw near to God through bringing about social change. This desire is so strong that many activists would explain their *worship* as standing and fighting against evil along with calling sinners to repentance. When they stand against injustice and evil, they believe they are working in cooperation and partnership with God. These are the people who hear of an injustice and feel closest to God when working toward change and fighting for the oppressed.

6. Caregivers: Love and connect with God by loving others

Caregivers love God and experience His presence when they are loving and serving others. They are drawn to the poor, needy, and sick. They are usually the first ones to meet a felt physical need like a meal or a ride or volunteer to help in other ways. Caregivers' faith is experienced as helping others. They usually jump in to meet needs—they are doers. Their faith has to come from action and service to others, not just simply talking or singing about their love for God.

7. Enthusiasts: Love and connect with God through mystery and celebration

Enthusiasts tend to experience God through exuberance and celebration. They are seen as the cheerleaders of the faith. Their love for God is experienced through shouting *amen*, dancing in the aisles, and worshiping God with joyful celebration. They experience God's love, power, and presence best when their hearts are moved and they feel His presence.

8. Contemplatives: Love and connect with God through adoration

Contemplatives adore, cherish, worship, and admire God. They seek God's presence and love. Contemplatives are drawn to God when their emotions are awakened, and they sense God touching their heart and speaking words of love and affection to them. While they may serve God and *do* things on His behalf, their focus is on seeking to love God with a pure and deep love. Many times contemplatives want to be alone with God through prayer and silence.

9. Intellectuals: Love and connect with God through the mind

Intellectuals are moved and drawn to a world of concepts and ideas. They need to know and understand what they believe. They are drawn to community and churches that define and maintain proper doctrine. You will likely find them studying and sometimes debating doctrine and theology and ideas. Intellectuals feel closest to God's love and presence when they are learning something new about Him that they didn't understand before, especially when they are given time to study Scripture or theology books (Gary 2000).

We all connect to God in different ways that are based in how God made us. Each of us is "fearfully and wonderfully made" (Psalm 139:14 NIV). We rekindle hope and maintain self-care during time with friends, family, and God. We can define *hope* as a confident expectation. The wounds of our past and the stress of our present can destroy hope. I have been pondering for several years about the end of Corinthians 13, the love chapter. "And now these three remain: faith, hope and love. But the greatest of these is love" (1 Corinthians 13:13 NIV). I understand the importance of faith because we can't please God without faith (see Hebrews 11:6). The entire chapter of 1 Corinthians 13 describes how important love is. The interesting part is hope—it is as important as faith and love. Life without hope is empty, frustrating, and unfulfilling. The heart of self-care is creating and maintaining hope.

Self-care takes determination and willpower to face the stress of our normal chaotic life. Healthy self-care offers a new way of seeing what is in front of us and allows us to learn from what we have experienced. Learn to practice self-care that will bring a new perspective and hope that things could be different.

The payoff of self-care can be very rewarding. Self-care that produces hope is never a static or passive thing. It is dynamic, on the move. It takes work that you need to make a priority. The hope that healthy self-care produces gives peace and joy even in the midst of turmoil, courage and confidence instead of fear. Caring for your body, soul, and spirit helps you to have gratitude in a negative world.

Why are we putting all this focus on gratitude? You have to choose what you focus on. Stress, trauma, and our busy lives make focus and concentration harder. To get rid of your negative racing thoughts, you have to have another thought. Gratitude is the thought you need to pull yourself back to. Gratitude is important because it can change everything. Think about it. Gratitude transforms the way you interact in your relationships. It fills the empty glass of your emotions. Gratitude truly is able to say, "God has worked all things together for my good!"

In our day-to-day lives the tendency is to notice the negative. We get caught up in the things that go wrong and feel as though we're living under our own private rain cloud. The concern is that we don't notice the positive. We tend to adapt and absorb the good things and people in our lives, taking them for granted. The result is that we often overlook everyday beauty and goodness—a kind gesture from a friend or the warmth of our partner on a chilly morning. In the process we miss opportunities for happiness and connection.

At the end of each day try to recall three positive things that happened. Take the time to notice them and thank God. Don't look for just the big things; acknowledge the small things, like the giggle of your child or the beauty of a sunrise or sunset. Train yourself to notice beauty and goodness. You will be surprised at what God brings into your life daily. So often we are too worried, stressed, and anxious to notice. End your day counting the blessings, not dwelling on the anxiety and worry of the negative.

This practice guards against the tendency to notice only the negative. By remembering and listing three positive things that have happened in your day—and maybe even considering what caused them—you tune into the sources of goodness in your life. It's a habit that can change the emotional tone of your life, replacing feelings of disappointment or entitlement with those of gratitude, which may be why this practice is associated with significant increases in happiness.

Healthy self-care can motivate us to seize each day and not just go through the motions with no expectations of change. Over the years I have tried to understand that the only thing I can control is me. I am learning to let go and find hope again. *I have one hundred percent control of myself and zero percent control of anything else.* That statement is designed to give you peace, not fear or anxiety. Something larger and greater than you is in control; it is safe to let go. This chaotic world we all live in causes us to react by gripping and controlling. You don't find life that way. You find life by letting go and acknowledging that God is in control, and you are secure in His love.

References

Contrada, R. J., and A. Baum, eds. 2010. *The Handbook of Stress Science: Biology, Psychology, and Health.* New York: Springer.

DiGiuseppe, R. A. and K. Doyle. 2001. "Rational Emotive Behavior Therapy." In *Handbook of Cognitive-Behavioral Therapies,* ed. K. S. Dobson, 3rd ed., 226–76. New York: Guilford Press.

Dutcher, J. M. 2012. "Improving Performance on a Creativity Task via Self-Affirmation." *Carnegie Mellon University Research Showcase.* Pittsburgh. 1–23.

Emmons, R. A., M. E. McCullough. 2003. "Counting Blessings Versus Burdens: An Experimental Investigation of Gratitude and Subjective Well-being in Daily Life." *Journal of Personality and Social Psychology,* February, 84 no. 2, 377–89.

Harvard Health Publications. 2006. "Six for 2006: Six Reasons Not to Scrimp on Sleep." *Harvard Women's Health Watch,* 13 no. 5, 1–3. http://www.tamaqua.k12.pa.us/625870111611241/lib/625870111611241/sleep.pdf.

He, S. B., W. G. Tang, W. J. Tang, X. L. Kao, C. G. Zhang, and X. T. Wong. 2012. "Exercise Intervention May Prevent Depression." *International Journal of Sports Medicine,* 33 no. 7, 525–30.

Lakhan, S. E., & K. F. Vieira. 2008. "Nutritional Therapies for Mental Disorders." *Nutrition Journal* 7, no. 2, 1–8.

"How Expressive Writing Promotes Health and Emotional Well-Being." 2002. In *The Writing Cure: How Expressive Writing Promotes Health and Emotional Well-being.* S. J. Lepore and J. M. Smythe, eds. Washington, D.C: American Psychological Association.

Mayo Clinic. 2019. "Chronic stress puts your health at risk." https://www.mayoclinic.org/healthy-lifestyle/stress-management/in-depth/stress/art-20046037#:~:text=The%20long%2Dterm%20activation%20of,Depression.

Miller, M. C. 2011. *Understanding Depression.* Boston: Harvard Medical School.

National Board for Certified Counselors. 2012. http://www.nbcc.org/OurCertifications

National Sleep Foundation. 2008. "Longer Work Days Leave Americans Nodding Off on the Job." http://www.sleepfoundation.org/article/press-release/longer-work-days-leave-americans-nodding-the-job.

Ong, A. D., A. J. Zautra, and M. C. Reid. 2010. "Psychological Resilience Predicts Decreases in Pain Catastrophizing Through Positive Emotions." *Psychol Aging.* September 25. no. 3, 516–23.

Payne, R. A., and M. Donaghy. 2010. *Relaxation Techniques: A Practical Handbook for the Health Care Professional,* 4th ed. Edinburgh: Churchill Livingstone.

Pennebaker, J. W. 1997. *Opening Up: The Healing Power of Expressing Emotions.* New York: Guildford Press.

Pratt, L. A., D. J. Brody, and Q. Gu. 2011. "Antidepressant Use in Persons Aged 12 and Over: United States, 2005–2008." *NCHS Data Brief No. 76.* Hyattsville, Md. National Center for Health Statistics.

Rippe, J. M. 2018. "Lifestyle Medicine: The Health Promoting Power of Daily Habits and Practices." *Am J Lifestyle Med.* 12 no. 6, 499–512.

Sathyanarayana Rao, T. S., M. R. Asha, B. N. Ramesh, and K. S. Jagannatha Rao. 2008. "Understanding Nutrition, Depression and Mental Illnesses." *Indian J Psychiatry* April–June, 50 no. 2, 77–82.

Seligson, S. 2010. "Exercise: The Other Antidepressant." http://www.bu.edu/today/2010/exercise-the-other-antidepressant/.

Thomas, Gary. 2000. *Sacred Pathways.* Grand Rapids, Mich.: Zondervan Publishing.

Tripp, P. D. 2014. *New Morning Mercies: A Daily Gospel Devotional.* Wheaton, Ill.: Crossway.

Uchino, B. N., D. Uno, and J. Holt-Lunstad. 1999. "Social Support, Physiological Processes, and Health." *Current Directions in Psychological Science,* 8 no. 5, 145–48.

Vandyck, P., R. Chadband, B. Chaudhary, and M. E. Stachura. 1989. "Sleep Apnea, Sleep Disorders, and Hypothyroidism." *American Journal of the Medical Sciences,* 298 no. 2, 119–22.

Made in the USA
Columbia, SC
06 June 2021

39258330R00076